Storytelling Made Easy
with Puppets

Storytelling Made Easy with Puppets

by Jan M. VanSchuyver

Illustrated by Ellen Kae Hester

9311872

ORYX PRESS
1993

The rare Arabian Oryx is believed to have inspired the myth of the unicorn. This desert antelope became virtually extinct in the early 1960s. At that time several groups of international conservationists arranged to have 9 animals sent to the Phoenix Zoo to be the nucleus of a captive breeding herd. Today the Oryx population is nearly 800, and over 400 have been returned to reserves in the Middle East.

Photograph on the back cover by Andrew Kilgore

Copyright © 1993 by
The Oryx Press
4041 North Central at Indian School Road
Phoenix, Arizona 85012-3397

Published simultaneously in Canada

Printed and Bound in the United States of America

∞ The paper used in this publication meets the minimum requirements of American National Standard for Information Science—Permanence of Paper for Printed Library Materials, ANSI Z39.48, 1984.

Library of Congress Cataloging-in-Publication Data

VanSchuyver, Jan M.
    Storytelling made easy with puppets / by Jan M. VanSchuyver;
illustrated by Ellen Kae Hester.
        p.   cm.
    Includes bibliographical references (p.   ) and index.
    ISBN 0-89774-732-1
    1. Puppet plays.   2. Puppet theater—United States.   3. Hand
puppets—United States.   I. Title.
PN1980.V36   1993
791.5'3—dc20   92-45900
                                                CIP

Contents

Contents

Preface

Puppetry can be very simple and yet still remain full of magic, wonder, and the power to bring stories to life. Puppetry can be effective even in the hands of people who cannot spontaneously think of a thing to say or do with a puppet.

This book provides step-by-step instructions for people who want to use puppets with literature for children ages two to eight. Because it contains well-known classics and unusual ideas, it will be useful to both beginning and experienced puppeteers and storytellers. Children's librarians, preschool and elementary school teachers, storytellers, school librarians, day-care providers, Sunday school teachers, recreation leaders, teacher's aides, parents, and even therapists and counselors will find it to be a valuable resource.

Anyone who wants to become a puppeteer and is willing to give a minimal amount of time to planning and practice can be very successful with puppets. This book contains all the information necessary to learn to use puppets with children.

It is not necessary to read the entire book before beginning to use puppets. A few basic guidelines presented in the introduction to Section One combine with any of the scripts given to provide everything needed for a successful puppet presentation. Within each chapter, the easiest activities are listed first.

Section One contains 24 scripts with complete directions for successful activities that use puppets to bring literature to life. All of the scripts are structured to be performed by one adult, using puppets without a stage, making puppetry practical to use in many different situations and settings. This section includes ten scripts for storytelling with puppets, five scripts for leading songs with puppets, and nine scripts for using puppets to introduce and follow up stories.

Section Two features seven simple puppet activities children can do. These activities work well as follow-up activities to puppet presentations made by adults using the scripts in Section One. Involving children in acting out stories with puppets is a valuable whole language activity. Storytelling builds excitement for literature and directly involves children with story structure as well as with oral and written language. Chapter 6 lists group projects, and Chapter 7 contains plans that allow a child to learn a story and create all the puppets needed to tell the story individually.

Section Three gives more information on puppetry and storytelling for people who have used some of the scripts and want to know and do more. Chapter 8 focuses on common problems and their solutions. Refer to it for help using the ideas in the scripts and for more information on puppet manipulation, voice development, and performance. Chapter 9 has an extensive list of children's literature, arranged by themes that correspond to the themes of the scripts in Section One. In addition to being listed by theme, the entries give age range to assist the reader in quickly finding additional age-appropriate literature to use with puppets. Chapter 10 lists sources for purchasing puppets to be used with these scripts as well as for other puppet activities. It also provides a selected bibliography of books for adults on puppetry and storytelling and a list of storytelling and puppetry organizations and resources.

Acknowledgments

Many people helped make this book possible. To those named below and more, I am grateful.

Judy Sierra and Robert Kaminski, for their continuing friendship and creative support.

Lilian Bern, for moral support, dinners, and rephrasing when the words wouldn't come.

Toni Langfield, for her fountain of ideas and encouragement.

Howard Batchelor, whose gentle persistence got me to shut up and write.

Pam Wade, for great brainstorming sessions.

Molly McDermott, for showing me that "The Three Billy Goats Gruff" can be effectively performed with only one goat puppet.

Auburn-Placer County Library staff, for cheerful help with my research.

All my friends and colleagues in the fields of puppetry and storytelling who are so generous with their knowledge.

And especially to my students of the past 15 years who have believed and blossomed in the magic of storytelling and puppetry.

Section One:
<u>Scripts</u>

Chapter One
Introduction

Read this chapter before using the scripts. It will give you valuable guidance as you enter the world of puppetry and storytelling.

The scripts in this section are divided into four chapters. Chapter 2 focuses on using puppets to introduce any book. If you are a beginner who hasn't used puppets before, using a puppet to introduce a book is an easy way to start. Chapter 3 explains ways to introduce specific books using specific puppets. Chapter 4 shows how to use puppets to lead songs, and Chapter 5 presents storytelling with puppets. Within the chapters, the easier scripts are listed first, and so you may want to try these first and build up to the more difficult scripts as your confidence grows.

In using all the scripts that follow, keep these vital tips in mind:

1. The audience is watching the puppet, not the puppeteer.

Sometimes, when using a puppet without a stage, the puppeteer is afraid of looking silly. The solution to this concern is for the puppeteer to focus on the puppet, rather than on himself or herself. At some point during the performance, notice where the attention of the audience is focused—not on the puppeteer, but on the puppet. Then just remember that no one is looking at you, the puppeteer, anyway. Be bold, have fun, and enjoy the puppet and the material. If you do, your audience will, too.

2. Keep the puppet "alive" for the audience.

Remember to treat the puppet as if it has thoughts and feelings of its own at all times. Your puppet has a brain! As long as you have the puppet in view of the audience, you have to have at least part of your attention on keeping that puppet "alive" for the audience. To assist you in maintaining the illusion of puppet "life," don't let your audience see you put your puppet on or take it off to lie lifeless as you begin the next activity. It is vital that the puppet remain "alive" when it is in view.

The puppet does not always have to be the center of attention, however. The puppet can be kept "alive" while resting in your arms by "breathing" and looking at you as you give the children some instructions. If you want the children's attention on you, the puppet's attention should also be on you. The puppet's focus will encourage the children to give you at least part of their attention. They will also be watching the puppet in anticipation of what it might do next.

When you manipulate the puppet, be aware that it is governed by the same laws of gravity that we are. Use your body as a puppet stage whenever you can to keep the illusion of the puppet as a being affected by gravity. For example, have the puppet sit on your arm as it talks to the children and have it sleep against your shoulder rather than in thin air. Even if you are making the bunny hop along in the air, create the illusion of gravity by keeping it a consistent level from the ground as it moves forward. Additional information on puppet movement is listed in Chapter 8.

A shopping bag is a great puppet living space.

3. Have a good place for your puppet to be out of sight when not in use.

The necessity of having part of your mind on the puppet at all times when it is visible to the audience makes it imperative that you have a place for the puppet to be easily put out of sight when you are finished using it. A puppet hiding/living space should be easy to obtain, preferably inexpensive, and lightweight. Also, it should be easy to store, taking up a small amount of space when not being used.

One of my favorite puppet storage spaces is a shopping bag. I buy brightly colored bags with handles, stocking up at Christmas time with enough bags to last throughout the year. Some gift stores carry them all year as well. These bags are great because they are lightweight, inexpensive, and easy to carry and store.

When the puppet is out of sight in its bag, our imaginations can "see" it doing any number of things. This possibility was shown to me by a second-grade class when Max the Monster and I had finished doing the "Peanut Butter/Jelly!" song with them. The children were *very* reluctant to see Max go. But because our time together was up, and because I was still at the stage in my puppet career of only doing what I had pre-planned and then putting the puppet away, I insisted that Max had to go back into his bag.

The children agreed, but they wanted to make sure he was comfortable in there! They asked questions like "Does he have a blanket in there? What if he gets hungry? Is he scared of the dark?" I saw that Max's bag could, and should, become his home. Now Max's bag always contains a very realistic-looking peanut butter and jelly sandwich made of foam, as well as a paperback copy of his favorite book, *Where the Wild Things Are* by Maurice Sendak. In our imaginations, however, it contains much more.

If the children are worried about him being lonely or bored in his bag, Max brings out his book or sandwich to show them what he'll be doing in there. Our imaginations can "see" him in there reading his book, eating his sandwich (hopefully without getting peanut butter and jelly everywhere), listening intently to the book or story he has introduced that I am now telling the children, taking a nap, or whatever is appropriate at the time.

The same atmosphere for puppet life can be created in many other convenient spaces, including the teacher's desk drawer; a papier mâché tree stump for a wild animal collection; a puppet apron with big, comfortable pockets for small puppets; a cardboard box doghouse for a puppy puppet; and a basket with a lid for a bunny puppet.

Hand Puppet

4. Choose a puppet that works well for the task at hand.

Chapter 10 lists sources for purchasing commercial puppets. You may also wish to explore books on puppet making if you need to create a particular character for a favorite story or song. A list of such books also appears in Chapter 10.

I prefer to use hand puppets, finger puppets, pop-up puppets, or rod puppets for these scripts. They do not require any special lighting or staging, and because they are close to the puppeteer's body, they work well in this intimate setting where the puppeteer's body often becomes the stage.

Hand puppets fit directly onto the puppeteer's hand. Overall, I find them the most versatile and satisfying type of puppet for these scripts, although they may be a bit more difficult to operate for some beginners. The advantages of all the recommended types of puppets are discussed in the following paragraphs.

There are basically two different types of hand puppets—those with moving mouths and those without. Hand puppets with moving mouths usually have the puppeteer's thumb in the lower jaw and the fingers in the upper part of the mouth. This setup allows the puppeteer to make the puppet's mouth move as it talks and to use the puppet's mouth to pick up objects. Sometimes a more complex arrangement of fingers inside allows the puppeteer to control arms, or front legs if it's an animal, as well as to move the mouth. This more complex arrangement usually requires more practice than just moving the mouth.

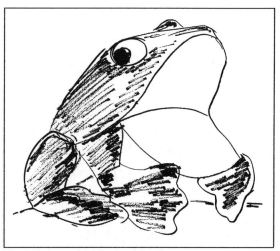

Hand Puppet with Moving Mouth

Hand puppets without moving mouths usually have the puppeteer's index finger and perhaps middle finger also in the head, with the thumb in one arm and the remaining fingers in the other arm. This arrangement allows the puppet to pick up books with its hands, as the puppeteer's fingers and thumb are inside to control them. This puppet generally nods its head and/or gestures appropriately to indicate when it is talking.

Finger puppets are small enough to slip onto a puppeteer's finger or thumb. Useful for small groups where everyone can see a small figure, they have the advantage of traveling in a pocket or purse to be available at a moment's notice. Their movements are somewhat limited. They cannot pick up things, although they can pretend to do so as you will see in "The Teeny Tiny Woman" script in this book. (See page 58.)

Finger Puppet

5

Pop-up Puppet

Pop-up puppets appear and disappear from their cone-shaped houses as you pull on the stick. They are simple to operate and fascinating to young children. The one disadvantage is that they also are unable to pick up things.

Rod puppets or stick puppets can be large enough to be seen by a large audience, and they can be quick and easy for children and adults to make. They are easy to manipulate but also have the disadvantage of often being unable to pick up things. More complex rod puppets exist but are beyond the scope of discussion in this book.

I do not like using shadow puppets and marionettes for the scripts in this book. Shadow puppets need special lighting and staging that requires more setup and also keeps the storyteller or song leader out of view of the audience. Marionettes, also called string puppets, are often difficult to see unless the puppeteer is on some type of elevated stage. Also, both shadow puppets and marionettes are unable to pick up everyday objects, like books, unless they are special puppet props.

Stick Puppet or Rod Puppet

5. Experiment before deciding on which hand to wear your puppet.

If you are right-handed and the script only calls for one puppet, you will probably want to wear the puppet on your right hand. If the script calls for two puppets, often one of the puppets will have more difficult movements than the other. Try the characters first on one hand, then the other, to find the most effective arrangement for each script you use.

6. Beginning puppeteers will want to start small.

As you begin using puppets, use a script from the book to plan exactly what you will do with the puppet, do that, and promptly put the puppet away. This will work very well, and you will not have that uncomfortable feeling of "what do I do with this puppet now that I've brought it out here."

The more positive experiences you have using puppets, the easier it will be for you to bring them to life. It is only through using puppets that you will become familiar with what makes them effective for you and with children. Once you have successfully done some of the activities with puppets presented here, you also may find yourself spontaneously thinking of more things your puppets can do.

After about two years of planning what I would do with the puppet and staying faithful to my plans, I began to have ideas on the spot of things the puppet and I could do. These ideas occurred occasionally at first and then with increasing frequency as I gained more experience and confidence.

The first time this happened, I was using a cowboy on a horse to lead the song "Chisolm Trail." When the song was complete, the preschoolers had enjoyed it so much that I was reluctant to put the puppet away. Suddenly I had an idea! Actually, it felt more like the children encouraged the puppet to have the idea.

The cowboy's horse could count, showing the numbers by swishing its tail. (Because it had no feet, it could not use the more traditional method of stamping the ground once for each number.) I asked the children to challenge the horse. They called out numbers, carefully counting the tail swishes to be sure the horse got it right, giggling when they had to help him, and getting some counting practice themselves along with the fun. Now the horse has also learned simple addition and subtraction, with the help of children in the audience.

Whether you work strictly with the ideas found here, or also develop additional puppet routines on your own and by using other puppetry books, you will find yourself successful in the creative, imaginative, and playful world of puppetry. So get started!

Chapter Two
Using Any Hand Puppet Character to Introduce Any Book

In this chapter, the scripts show how to use any hand puppet character to introduce any book. You may wish to choose one of your puppets to be the storytime helper and use this puppet only for this task. This puppet may participate in every storytime or only on special occasions. Maybe on Fridays the children are generally more restless, so the puppet helper comes to storytime every Friday.

A puppet can easily capture and direct the attention of your audience. This can be used advantageously at the beginning of storytime to focus the children and create anticipation for the stories they will hear.

Puppets can also be used during storytime to simply introduce the next story. The silly business your puppet can produce will allow the children a short break from the concentrated attention required when listening to a story. The puppet can give the children an opportunity to laugh, talk, and wiggle a bit between books before focusing their attention on the next story or activity to be presented. Children of all ages respond well to this kind of a break.

For my storytime helper, I use Mortimer, a commercially made, friendly looking bear puppet. Mortimer is a hand puppet with a moving mouth and a very expressive face. Although he has arms and legs, they are stuffed and not controlled by fingers. Therefore, he picks up books and brings them to me in his mouth. If your hand puppet does not have a moving mouth, it can still be used as a storytime helper if it is able to pick up books using its hands or paws.

During storytime, Mortimer stays in an old trunk, the same trunk where I also keep the books for storytime. The children know that his main job is to help keep the books in order and bring me particular books as I ask him for them. A large shopping bag or a decorated cardboard box with a lid that is easy to open and close could serve the same purpose as my story trunk.

One note of caution: If more than one teacher uses the story trunk, and only you use a puppet during storytime, it is important to make it clear to the children that the puppet actually lives with you, not in the trunk.

When one of my colleagues did storytime in my absence one day, the children *insisted* that Mortimer lived in the trunk. They wanted to see him! She finally had to show them that he wasn't inside the trunk, and they were very disappointed. *Now* they know that Mortimer goes home with me, and he does not come to storytime without me.

The scripts that follow describe specifically how you can use any hand puppet character able to pick up a book in its mouth or with its arms to introduce books during storytime. The scripts call the puppet Mortimer because it sounds less awkward than saying the puppet; feel free to use your own puppet name.

Mortimer peeks out at the children from inside the story trunk, building their anticipation for whatever he will do next.

BOOK TOO HEAVY

"Book Too Heavy" is a fast bit of business guaranteed to produce lots of giggles. Do this one with an extra large picture book, such as *More, More, More Said the Baby* by Vera Williams.

What to Say	**What to Do**
The next book I'm going to read is (state the title).	Look inside the story trunk or bag as you reach in and put Mortimer on your hand.
Would you please bring it out for me, Mortimer?	Mortimer's head peeks over the top of the story trunk lid, he nods "yes," and disappears into the trunk. Leave the lid open. With your hand still inside Mortimer, make some crashing sounds inside the trunk.
What's the matter, Mortimer, having trouble?	Look in again as you speak to him . . . Mortimer's head reappears over the top of the trunk lid. He nods "yes," more vigorously this time, and disappears again. Make more crashing sounds. Look at the children, then back into the trunk.
Here, Mortimer, maybe I can help you get ahold of the book. There, you have it. Bring it up for us. Pull . . . pull	Lean over the trunk and reach in with your free hand to help. Mortimer's ears and the top of his head slowly appear above the trunk lid.
Ohhhhh!	Abruptly they disappear, and crashing sounds are heard again.
Gosh, Mortimer, that big book got away from you.	React with lots of surprise, looking into the trunk and then at the children.
Here, let me help you get ahold of it again. Now you can do it. Bring it up for us. Pull . . . pull . . . pull	Again, lean over the trunk and reach in with your other hand to help. Mortimer's ears and more of his head slowly appear above the trunk lid. Everyone can see that Mortimer has a book in his mouth.
Oh, no!	Abruptly he disappears again, and even louder crashing sounds are heard.
Mortimer, I do believe that book pulled you right back into the trunk!	React with more surprise.
May I help you with the book?	Look into the trunk as you speak to Mortimer. Mortimer's face reappears, and he nods solemnly.

9

Together, I know we can do it! Here it comes . . . keep on pulling. Don't give up.

Together, you and Mortimer muscle the book out of the trunk. The book almost pulls Mortimer back in a few times, but you both hang on.

There, we got it!

Once the book is in your lap, Mortimer sits on the top of the trunk lid for a minute, panting.

Mortimer, thank you for your help in bringing this big storybook out here.

Mortimer takes a slight bow, still panting from his efforts with the book.

You really deserve a rest now. Go on down into the trunk and get comfy.

Mortimer wearily goes down into the trunk. Look into the trunk as you make sure he is comfortable.

You can listen to the story in there.

Close the lid to the trunk and begin to read the book to the children.

CAN'T FIND BOOK

"Can't Find Book" involves the children in helping Mortimer, or whatever your puppet's name is, find the right book. If they know what the book looks like already, they can give Mortimer feedback when he brings up the wrong one. In this example, you lead them by describing the book and by asking appropriate questions when Mortimer appears. The script works for any books, not just the ones listed here. Alter your descriptions to go with the books you're using.

What to Say

What to Do

Mortimer, would you bring out the next book for us, please.

Look inside the story trunk. As you speak, reach in and put Mortimer on your hand. Make Mortimer peek over the lid of the trunk, so that you and the children can see him.

Remember, we are going to read the book called *Harry, the Dirty Dog.*

Mortimer nods and disappears into the story trunk. You all hear some crashing and banging around inside the trunk.

Mortimer, what's the matter?

Look at the children and then back into the trunk.

Try to move quickly, Mortimer. We're all waiting for you.

Quickly Mortimer pops out holding *Whistle for Willie* in his mouth.

Well, Mortimer, that book does have a dog on the cover, but Harry is a white dog with black spots. Girls and boys, is that (pointing to the dog on the cover of *Whistle for Willie*) a white dog with black spots?

Children answer "no," and Mortimer nods solemnly in agreement.

Go ahead and try again, Mortimer.

Mortimer returns to the trunk and does some more crashing around. You look back into the trunk.

Any luck in there, Mortimer?

Mortimer brings out a book about bathtime.

I see, Mortimer, you thought if the story was about a dirty dog it might have baths in it.

Mortimer nods "yes," still holding the book in his mouth.

Well, you are right, but the book we want has a picture of Harry on the cover. Boys and girls, do you see Harry anywhere on the cover of this book?

Again, children answer "no," and Mortimer nods solemnly in agreement. He returns to the trunk.

Girls and boys, do you think Mortimer will find it this time? I hope so!	**Finally he reappears with *Harry, the Dirty Dog*.**
Boys and girls, do you think this is the book we've been waiting for?	**Probably some will answer "yes" and some will answer "no."**
Look at the dog on the front of the book. What color is he?	**The children will answer your question about the color of the dog. Mortimer nods happily as you take the book from him.**
You found Harry!	
Thank you so much, Mortimer. You went on a very careful search to find this book for us. Boys and girls, let's give Mortimer a hand for his good work.	**Children clap; Mortimer bows.**
Now you may go back into the story trunk and lie down to rest while I read this story. If you're very quiet in your trunk, you'll be able to hear the story, too.	**Mortimer goes back into the trunk. When he's settled, and off your hand, close the lid of the trunk, turn toward the children, and start the story.**

BOOK UPSIDE DOWN

"Book Upside Down" can be very silly. Use it when the children really need a break and a chance to laugh and participate in the action.

What to Say	**What to Do**
Mortimer, I hope you are ready to help.	**As you speak, look inside the story trunk and put Mortimer on your hand, ready to come out.**
Would you please bring out the next book for us?	**Mortimer promptly comes out, holding a book in his mouth. The book is upside down and backwards, so the children cannot see the front cover.**
Thank you, Mortimer, but the children cannot see what the story is. Could you fix the book so they can see?	**Mortimer looks down at the book he is holding, tips his head to one side for a second as if he's thinking about the problem, and then carefully turns the book sideways with the back cover of the book still facing the audience. Help him accomplish this task by holding the book while he moves his mouth to a different part of the book to turn it.**
Children, can you tell what story this is now?	**The children will usually giggle and say "no!"**
Can you tell Mortimer what is wrong with the book?	**Children will usually respond with "It's sideways!" When they do, Mortimer lets go of the book for a moment to back up slightly and open his mouth in astonishment. Help him do this by holding the book in the same position he's been holding it.**
What could Mortimer do to fix it?	**Children respond, "Turn it around." Mortimer manages to turn the book all the way around without turning the front toward the children. When he stops, he looks toward the children, and then at you to see if it's right. The book is again upside down with its back cover still toward the audience.**
Oh, Mortimer.	**You will sound a bit hopeless at this point. Usually the children have dissolved into giggles. Mortimer hangs his head dejectedly.**

What should he do now to fix it?

Whatever the children suggest, try to have Mortimer perform the suggestions without actually turning the book right side up with the front cover facing the audience. Variations on this silliness include Mortimer turning the book around so the front cover is facing forward and the book is still upside down. He can then turn the book sideways, and the children can point out to him that they still cannot read the title. Mortimer has also been known to become so frustrated that he places the book flat on your lap and just sits on it.

Of course, when you are ready to end this stretcher and get on with the story, Mortimer can finally triumph and hold the book right side up with the cover facing front. Lots of praise and applause is due Mortimer at that point, and he deserves a long rest in the story trunk while the children hear the story.

GETTING DRESSED FOR STORYTIME

"Getting Dressed for Storytime" can be used to introduce many different books and many different occasions. By changing your puppet's clothes, you expand the range of things your puppet can talk about and demonstrate for the children. You will not need a new puppet each time to introduce a new idea or new story. You can use your familiar storytime puppet wearing new clothes.

Often you can find very inexpensive, effective clothing for your puppet at thrift stores. Look in the infant clothing section as well as in the toy section. Most puppets large enough for adult hands will be able to wear human infant clothes. Hats and bibs are effective because you can easily put them on and take them off. Shirts that open down the front are sometimes easier to get on your puppet than those that pull on, depending on the size of your puppet's head. If your puppet has legs and you can find pants to fit, make a slit in the seat of the pants corresponding to the hole in the bottom of the puppet where your arm goes.

As you introduce the book, your puppet can wear an article of clothing found in the story, or your puppet can wear an article of clothing to help introduce a concept found in the book. For example, a Hawaiian shirt could help you to introduce a book on Hawaii; a red muffler could introduce a theme of winter or colors. The script that follows gives detailed ideas for using a knit hat to capture the audience's attention and to generate discussion on a concept found in the story. This script describes using a puppet with feet. If your puppet has no feet, the hat can appear on one arm and then the other before appearing on its head.

See Chapter 9 under "Clothes" for a list of stories with clothes as their theme. These books can also be enhanced, using variations on the idea listed below.

What to Say	**What to Do**
Mortimer, are you ready to come out and help me tell the children about the next story?	Look into the story trunk and pull Mortimer's knit cap on over his feet. Then bring him up so only his head is visible and have him look at you and nod "yes."
Well, come on out, then.	Mortimer hops out and sits on your arm, looking at the children.
Mortimer, what are you wearing?	Speak to him in an astonished tone as you and he both look down at the knit cap on his feet.
I do believe that is your hat!	Mortimer nods "yes" quite vigorously, looking at you and then at the children.

Children, is Mortimer wearing his hat in the right place?

You and Mortimer look at the children expectantly, and most of them call out "no." Mortimer backs up in astonishment.

Mortimer appears, wearing his hat on his feet.

Perhaps you can tell him where he should be wearing his hat.

Mortimer, go back into the trunk and put your hat on your head.

Direct your statement to the children. Most of them will call out "on his head!"

Look at Mortimer and then have Mortimer nod "yes" and hop out of sight into the trunk. Reach casually in with him and put his hat on his paw or arm or anyplace it will fit other than on his head.

Are you ready, Mortimer?

Again, bring him up so only his head is visible and have him look at you and nod "yes" before turning to look at the children.

Well, come on out, then.

Sound doubtful, because you can see that his hat is not on his head. Mortimer hops out and sits on your arm. You and the children giggle together as you see where Mortimer is wearing his hat.

Children, did Mortimer put his hat on his head this time?

Show the amusement in your voice as you ask the question. Both you and Mortimer look at the children as they answer "no!" Mortimer looks dejected by hanging his head and sighing a big sigh.

Mortimer, what is wrong?

Look at Mortimer. He whispers his answer in your ear because he is too embarrassed to speak out loud.

Mortimer is now wearing his hat on his arm.

13

Oh Mortimer, you are not sure where your head is? I'm sorry.

Speak gently with sympathy as he shakes his head "no."

Children, show Mortimer where your heads are.

You and Mortimer look at the children, who point to their heads.

Now do you think you can put your hat on *your* head, Mortimer?

Mortimer nods "yes" without much enthusiasm and hops back into the story trunk. Reach inside and help him pull his hat down over his head until his head is completely covered.

OK. Come out and show us your hat *on your head.*

Slowly Mortimer emerges from inside the story trunk and gropes his way to his customary seat on your arm.

Oh, Mortimer, you poor thing. No wonder you didn't want to put your hat there. You can't see!

Speak with sympathy. Mortimer nods his head "yes" from inside his hat.

Your hat is too big. Would you like me to help you fix it?

Again, Mortimer nods his head "yes" from inside his hat.

Mortimer's hat totally covers his head.

All right, Mortimer.

Keep Mortimer on your lap as you adjust his hat so that he can see. As Mortimer's hat is properly placed on his head, he opens his mouth wide in joy and astonishment. If your puppet does not have a moving mouth, you could have it jump up and down or clap its hands for joy.

There! That's better!

Mortimer nods "yes" with great enthusiasm.

Now that your hat is on straight, I want to ask the boys and girls something about it.

As you speak to Mortimer, look at him. Then you and Mortimer turn to look at the audience.

If you were going to wear a hat like this, what kind of weather would it be outside?

Children answer "cold!"

At this point, you may lead the discussion in the direction of the next story you plan to present. Remember, after Mortimer brings out the next book for you to read, it is easiest to settle him back into the story trunk out of sight. Just tell him if he's very quiet he'll be able to hear the story from his comfy bed inside the trunk.

Finally, Mortimer's hat is in the right place!

Four different ways the hat business could lead to introducing a book are listed here. Use one of the four ideas listed here to complete the script. You will probably begin to think of others as you use your storytime puppet with its new clothes.

1. And next I am going to share a story with you that takes place where it is very cold. Mortimer, now that you are properly dressed for the cold, please bring the next story out for us. (This could be any story that takes place in the winter or in a cold climate such as Alaska.)

2. You had a difficult time with your hat, Mortimer, and the next story is about a child who had a difficult time with some of his clothes, too. Would you please bring that story out so I can share it with the children? (See the stories listed in Chapter 9 under "Clothes" for ideas.)

3. Finally, Mortimer, you have your hat in place! The next story is about a man who wears not just one hat, but some brown, blue, gray, and red caps along with his own checkered cap! Please bring that story out for us, Mortimer. (Of course this is the introduction for the all-time favorite *Caps for Sale,* listed in Chapter 9 under "Clothes.")

4. So, children, does Mortimer have the kind of hat on that you might wear when you go on a picnic? (The children will usually respond that picnics happen in the summer when it is warm so Mortimer doesn't need his knit cap. They may also suggest that he might want a hat with a brim for shade.) Mortimer, bring out that story we have in the trunk about picnics, and we will see if anyone is wearing a hat like yours. (You may use *The Teddy Bears' Picnic*, listed in Chapter 9 under "Bears.")

Chapter Three
Using a Specific Puppet to Introduce a Specific Book

This chapter contains five scripts that demonstrate how specific puppet characters can both introduce and follow up specific stories. These characters have been chosen for their relevance to the books they introduce. For example, a little old woman puppet introduces *The Little Old Lady Who Was Not Afraid of Anything*.

SOMETHING TO CROW ABOUT

Story Source: Lane, Megan Halsey. *Something to Crow About.* New York: Dial Books for Young Readers, 1990.

Characters/Themes: Chickens, Self-esteem

Ages: 3 to 5

Story Summary: Cassie and Randall were young chicks who looked the same, but Cassie did everything better. She could scratch better, strut better, cheep better, and even find worms better. Poor Randall wanted to do just one thing better than Cassie. Finally Randall learns that he has a special talent, too, and Randall and Cassie learn to celebrate their differences.

The delightful pictures in this book are strong and clear enough to be seen by a classroom of kids gathered together for storytime.

Puppet Needed: You will need a rooster pop-up puppet. See Chapter 10 for information on where to purchase one. If you cannot find a rooster, buy a chicken and use it for a rooster in the story. The chicken has a beak and feathers. You may add a comb to make it look more like a rooster, if you wish.

Voice: For the story introduction, Randall the rooster is too shy to speak. He whispers in your ear, and you tell the children what he is saying. After the story, when Randall is showing off his crowing, he also speaks. He speaks with the energy and quickness of a crowing rooster. To help you keep his voice in mind, have him crow occasionally during the discussion. Read the section on puppet voices in Chapter 8 if you need more help finding and keeping Randall's voice.

Introduction

What to Say

Children, I have someone very special for you to meet. He lives in this yellow house.

Randall, the children are here. Come on out and say "hello."

Randall, I wanted you to come today because I have a surprise for you and the children.

I'm going to read a story about you and Cassie. Won't that be fun!

Randall, do come out.

Randall, please tell me what's wrong.

Randall says he doesn't want to come out and he really doesn't want to hear any stories about Cassie because she does everything better than he can. He doesn't like Cassie one bit!

What to Do

Reach into a bag, and bring out the pop-up puppet with his face concealed in the cone. During this routine, alternate between looking at Randall and looking at the children. Begin by looking at Randall's cone as you knock on the side of it and invite him to come out.

Randall pops out and looks around at the children.

Randall jumps up and down with excitement, looking at you and then at the children.

Randall looks at you, then at the children, then he slides back into his cone so only the top of his head and comb are showing. You look at the children in surprise.

Make Randall shake his head "no" without coming out or showing his face. The children can see his comb moving so they can tell he is shaking his head.

Slowly Randall peeks out of his cone just far enough to whisper in your ear. Then he disappears again.

Turn to the children as you tell them what he said.

Randall peeks out of his cone house. He refuses to come out because he does *not* want to hear any stories about Cassie.

Randall, you don't have to come out now if you don't want to. I do want you to listen to this story. You may be surprised at what you learn about yourself and about Cassie.

Look back to Randall's cone.

Will you at least listen?

Randall barely lifts his head up and down, showing very little of himself above the top of the cone.

Good. Make yourself comfortable here in this bag, and I will read the story to you and the girls and boys. Be sure to listen to all of it!

Put the puppet into the bag where he is out of sight, and then read the story.

Read *Something to Crow About.* After you finish the story, put the book aside and look into the bag, where Randall has been listening.

Follow-up

What to Say

Storyteller: Randall, are you ready to come out now?

What to Do

As you speak, reach in and bring out the puppet, with Randall still inside his cone.

The children have been waiting very patiently to see you again. Come on out.

Randall looks out and slowly turns his head to see all the children.

I'll bet they would like to hear you crow, just like you did in the story. Show us what you can do.

Randall pops to his full height and crows with enthusiasm.

Did that feel good, Randall?

Look at Randall.

Randall: It sure did!

He jumps up and down happily as he replies.

Storyteller: I'm glad you know that you have a special talent. No one else can crow just exactly like you do, can they?

Randall shakes his head "no."

And some creatures can't even crow at all.

Look at the audience as you say this line, then at Randall as he speaks.

Randall: Like Cassie!

Again, Randall jumps up and down happily.

Storyteller: That's right. Cassie has other special talents. And all these boys and girls out here have special talents, too.

Point toward the audience with your free hand.

Randall: They do?

Randall turns his head to look at all the boys and girls again.

Storyteller: Sure. Boys and girls, who can tell Randall about a special talent that you have or that one of your friends has?

Call on children who raise their hands.

At this point, as time permits, Randall could lead a discussion with the children about their strengths. Comments like "Joshua is good at singing," "Alice is good at building with the blocks," and "Cindy is a very fast runner" are encouraged. Randall responds to positive statements from the children by jumping up and down. He shows confusion by slowly sliding out of sight into his cone, to be coaxed out by the storyteller, who then helps the children explain what they mean to Randall. Throughout the discussion, Randall emphasizes that each person has something special to contribute.

DONNA O'NEESHUCK WAS CHASED BY SOME COWS

Story Source: Grossman, Bill. *Donna O'Neeshuck Was Chased by Some Cows*. Illustrated by Susan Truesdell. New York: Harper & Row, 1988.

Characters/Themes: Surprises, Animals

Ages: 3 to 8

Story Summary: Vigorous rhyming text matches the enthusiasm of Susan Truesdell's illustrations. Without knowing why, Donna O'Neeshuck is chased by a whole host of creatures, including cows, mooses, gooses, sows, cops, cats, a boy on a bike, and more. When she finally stops and asks them all what they want, she finds they want her to pat them on the head! It's a refreshing round of pure silliness with a message about sharing pats with your neighbors.

Puppet Needed: For this story you will need a cow hand puppet.

Voice: The cow's voice needs a hurried, breathless, frantic quality to it at first. It also should probably be in your lower vocal range, as a cow is a big animal with a fairly large and low voice. As the pats calm her down after the story, having her say "Mooo" occasionally will help you keep a lower, rounded, and contented cow tone to your voice when you speak for her. Use "Moooo" as a voice anchor. For more information on voice development, see Chapter 8.

Instructions: Sit on a low chair if the children are on the floor. If the children are in desks, sit on a stool high enough so that they can see your upper body as well as your face. Place a shopping bag containing the cow puppet either beside or behind you.

Introduction

What to Say

Storyteller: This bag holds the friend who came to tell us about the next story. Wait a minute while I bring her out.

Ms. Cow, what is the matter? Why are you running around so frantically?

What to Do

Reach into the bag and put the cow on your hand. While looking into the bag, wiggle the cow vigorously in the bag, making crashing sounds. Look at the children in surprise and then back to the bag as you swiftly bring the cow puppet out, having her run around in circles.

Continue the frantic movement. If you're sitting on a low chair, have the cow run around behind your back, run back out, run up and look over your left shoulder, etc. If you're sitting on a high stool, get up and run around in circles with the cow. Either way, you are creating the feeling of frantic activity with the cow. Finally, grab her with your free hand and settle her on your lap.

What to Say	What to Do
Ms. Cow: Mooo. I'm looking for Donna O'Neeshuck!	Ms. Cow looks at you as she answers.
Storyteller: Who, may I ask, is Donna O'Neeshuck?	Look at the children, surprised, and then back to the cow.
Ms. Cow: She's a girl, kind of skinny, with wild red hair and big eyes. Have you seen her?	Ms. Cow looks at you and then at the audience as she gives the description.
Storyteller: I don't know her. What is she wearing?	Look at the cow as you speak to her.
Ms. Cow: She's wearing blue jeans, a blue shirt, and red tennis shoes. She's a very fast runner!	As the cow answers, you and the cow alternate between looking at each other and out toward the audience.
Storyteller: I don't think I have seen anyone who exactly matches that description. Can you tell me why you are looking for her?	Shake your head "no" and look at the cow as you ask her the question.
Ms. Cow: No time for that! I have to keep looking!	Ms. Cow again begins running around frantically, finally running back into the bag.
Storyteller: Well, I have no idea what Ms. Cow is up to.	Take the puppet off and keep the bag in your hands as you speak to the children.
I do see a book in her bag that might help us solve the mystery. I hope she won't mind if I read it to you.	Reach into the bag and bring out the book, setting the bag behind you.

Read aloud *Donna O'Neeshuck Was Chased by Some Cows.*

Follow-up

What to Say

Storyteller: Now we know why Ms. Cow was looking for Donna O'Neeshuck. I'll bring her back out and see if she ever found her.

Ms. Cow, did you ever find Donna O'Neeshuck?

Ms. Cow: Moooooo. Keep doing that!

Storyteller: Doing what?

Ms. Cow: Mooooooo. Mooo. Patting my head! Head pats from you are very nice.

Storyteller: Are mine as good as Donna O'Neeshuck's?

Ms. Cow: Not quite. But *she* is missing, and you are here! Moooo. Mooo. Moo. Thank you.

What to Do

Pick up the bag and look inside as you reach in to put on the puppet. Speak to the cow while still looking into the bag.

Ms. Cow rattles the bag and again jumps out, running wildly and looking everywhere. Grab her with your free hand, hold her close, and calm her down by patting her head.

Through the next few exchanges, keep patting the cow's head and looking at her and then at the children watching.

She snuggles in contentedly.

Sound eager and hopeful.

She speaks gratefully.

This can be the end of the story, with the cow contentedly returning to her bag. If time permits, however, the puppet activity can continue with children from the audience patting the cow's head. A sample of how this could be handled follows.

Storyteller: I wonder if any of these girls and boys know how to give gentle head pats? Maybe you'd like some from them.

Look at the children and then back to the cow.

Ms. Cow: Mooo. Ohhhhh yes.

She nods "yes."

Storyteller: Children, if you'd like a chance to pat Ms. Cow's head, stay quietly in your places, and I will bring her to you for pats.

As you go around the group, remind them that Ms. Cow accepts only gentle pats from those who remain in their places. Each child who gives Ms. Cow a nice gentle pat on the head gets one in return from the cow. If Ms. Cow does not have a hoof with which to pat, she can pat the children with her chin. Children love this direct one-to-one contact with a puppet you have brought to life.

If anyone pats Ms. Cow too hard, have the puppet react by pulling away and hiding her head. Remind the children that Ms. Cow only likes gentle pats. If the child looks willing to be gentle, give him or her another chance to pat Ms. Cow. When everyone who wants to pat has had a turn, settle the puppet back into her bag with the following dialogue.

Storyteller: Ms. Cow, how are you feeling after all those wonderful pats?

Look at Ms. Cow.

Ms. Cow: Moooooo. Moooo. Marvelous.

She looks very relaxed.

Storyteller: I am so glad. You must be ready for a rest after running so hard looking for Donna O'Neeshuck. Let me settle you back into your bag.

Bring Ms. Cow's bag out.

Ms. Cow: Thank you so much.

Begin to put her away, but she peeks back out at you.

And thank all of you for those mooo, moo, marvelous pats. You are almost as good as Donna O'Neeshuck.

Have her turn to the children to thank them.

Storyteller: Good night, Ms. Cow.

Put her into the bag, put the bag away, and begin the next activity.

LIZARD'S SONG

Story Source: Shannon, George. *Lizard's Song.* Illustrated by Jose Aruego and Ariane Dewey. New York: Greenwillow Books, 1981.

Characters/Themes: Friends, Self-esteem, Bears

Ages: 3 to 8

Story Summary: Lizard was so happy with his life that he often made up songs. Bear liked one of Lizard's songs and wanted to learn it. Lizard very generously tried to teach Bear his song. Bear had a lot of trouble learning it and even more trouble remembering Lizard's song. Finally, Lizard realized that Bear needed a song of his own, and, with Lizard's help, Bear got one.

This very satisfying story has expressive illustrations clear enough to share with a group. The repeated song encourages audience participation.

Puppet Needed: A bear hand puppet could be used both to introduce this story and to lead singing and discussion following the story. Because Bear is very assertive and a little thick headed, try giving those characteristics to your bear puppet.

Voice: Bear's voice might be lower and a bit slower than your own speaking voice. Add a growly tone if you can do so comfortably. Be careful not to strain your vocal cords.

Introduction

What to Say	What to Do
Storyteller: Boys and girls, I have a friend here who is going to tell us something about the next story.	Bring Bear out of a shopping bag to introduce the story. He comes out a bit clumsily.
Bear: Hi, boys and girls. Can you guess what kind of creature is my best friend?	Allow the children to guess a few animals. Bear always responds with a positive comment about the animal mentioned. Unless someone guesses a lizard, Bear always says that the animal guessed is not the one. A sample exchange might go something like the one that follows.
Susie: Turtle!	
Bear: Well, I did have a turtle for a friend, once. And it was fun to have a friend who carried her house around on her back. But Turtle is not the friend I'm talking about now. Does anyone else have an idea?	Bear looks at the children as he replies. You may call on the children yourself or have Bear call on them.
Jason:: A wolf?	
Bear: You know, Jason, wolves do like to do what my best friend does. My best friend loves to sing, just like wolves love to howl. But my best friend is not a wolf. My best friend is a lizard.	
And in this bag I have a story about my best friend, Lizard, and me. Stay right there, and I'll show you the book. It's called *Lizard's Song*.	Bear disappears into the shopping bag and returns with the book.
Now I warn you that the bear in this book is blue, because the artist who made the pictures liked blue bears. Sometimes artists have fun like that. But even	Bear climbs back into the bag. Put the bag carefully to one side and a little behind you to discourage curious children from crawling up to look inside during the story.

though the bear is blue instead of brown, it is a story about *me*! I'm going into the bag to listen, and I'll come out after the story to see how you liked it.

Read *Lizard's Song* aloud, showing the children the illustrations.

Follow-up

Bear: Zoli zoli zoli . . . I just love that song! I'm so glad Lizard was willing to share it with me, and to help me make my own song, too.

When the story is finished, pick up the bag and bring Bear back out, singing.

If you were going to make a song for *you,* what would you sing?

Bear calls on a child and incorporates the child's idea into the song as he leads everyone in singing it.

Allow time for you and the children to sing several new verses of the song, trying to include all the types of places that children in the group might live. "House" is usually suggested first. Make sure that Bear does a verse with "apartment", and sometimes "trailer" or "tent" or "shelter" as well. You may also wish to sing songs for other animals. For example, you could sing "Hole is my home" for Rabbit and "Pond is my home" for Duck. The children really enjoy singing with Bear and creating their own songs based on the song in the story.

Similar Story: Another wonderful picture book with many similarities to *Lizard's Song* is the following Pueblo Indian tale:

Carey, Valerie Scho. *Quail Song.* New York: Putnam, 1990. Ages: 5 to 8. This delightful story of how Quail outwits the trickster Coyote is very accessible to children. Coyote walks by just as Quail cries "ki-ruu, ki-ruu" after cutting her finger. Coyote mistakes her cry for a song and insists that she teach it to him. In the ensuing action, Coyote literally bites off more than he can chew.

After reading *Lizard's Song* you may wish to share *Quail Song* with 5 to 8 year olds and discuss the similarities and differences between the two stories.

THE LITTLE OLD LADY WHO WAS NOT AFRAID OF ANYTHING

Story Source: Williams, Linda. *The Little Old Lady Who Was Not Afraid of Anything.* Illustrated by Megan Lloyd. New York: Crowell, 1986.

Characters/Themes: Self-esteem, Surprises, Scary Creatures

Ages: 2 to 7

Story Summary: A little old lady who is not afraid of anything is walking home alone through the forest on a dark night. On her way she meets some shoes, a pair of pants, a shirt, two white gloves, a tall black hat, and a very scary pumpkin head.

Although she is not afraid of anything, she is not foolish either, and each startling encounter causes her to walk a bit faster. After she meets the pumpkin head, she runs the rest of the way home, only to be surprised a bit later by a knock on her door. She answers it to find all the items floating in her doorway, still trying to scare her.

When the little old lady is still not afraid, the pumpkin head becomes unhappy and discouraged. Luckily, the old lady has an idea, which she whispers to the pumpkin. The next morning the old lady looks out her window to find all the items have taken her advice, joining together to create a scarecrow in her garden.

This is a perfect "scary" story for young children. It is a combination of the familiar and the strange presented with the reassuring rhythm and repetition that young children love. Megan Lloyd's deliciously scary illustrations are effective when shared with a group or with a single child.

Puppet Needed: You may use the same puppet to introduce this story that you use to tell "The Teeny Tiny Woman," a script also included in this book. (See page 58.) An old lady finger puppet, if your group is small enough to see it, or a hand puppet will work fine for this script.

Voice: If you want your voice to sound old, wrap your lower lip over your bottom teeth. When you do, it forces you to speak more slowly and articulate more carefully in order to be understood. You will sound a little like someone speaking without the dentures he or she normally wears. The more you curl your lip in around your teeth, the older you will sound. Add to this a slightly higher voice than your own speaking voice, and you will have a very effective voice for your old woman puppet.

Introduction

What to Say	**What to Do**
Old Lady: Hello, girls and boys. Today we are going to hear a s-c-a-a-a-r-y story.	Slowly bring the old lady puppet out of the bag you've placed in front of you. She may stand or sit on your other arm as she speaks to the children.

Discussion

Old Lady: How do you feel about scary stories?	Use the old lady puppet to lead a discussion about scary stories and experiences. Some sample questions are listed here.
Let's make a list of things that can be scary.	
What do you do if you are scared of something?	
All of us feel scared at times. I am glad it's time for the story. I think I'll go back into my bag where I can get comfortable and listen. Today's story is about a little old lady who was not afraid of anything.	After the children have had a chance to discuss these questions with the puppet, it is time for her to introduce the book.
	Have the puppet introduce the story and then climb back into her bag.

That's right! Not anything! I'll come back after the story is over to find out what you think of that.

She peeks out to add this final sentence and then disappears again. Place the bag beside your chair while you read the story.

Reading Suggestions

This story calls for careful timing to create just the right amount of suspense and scariness. Pause after you say the repeated line "But behind her she could hear . . ." and encourage the children to join in with you on the repeated list of noises made by the items the old woman meets on the dark road.

Follow-up

When the story is finished, pick up the bag and bring the old woman back out. Use her to lead a discussion of the children's feelings and ideas about the story. Be sure to emphasize that there are no wrong answers. Everyone has a right to his or her own opinion about the story's events. Suggested questions for the old lady to use are listed here.

> How did you feel when the old woman met those things on the road?
> How do you think she really felt when she saw the pumpkin head in the dark? Why?
> How do you think the pumpkin head, hat, gloves, shirt, pants, and shoes felt about the old woman's idea for them?

Old Lady: If you remember what all those things said as the old woman met them on the road in the dark, help me out by saying the sounds. Let's say the rhyme together one last time.

When you have finished with the discussion, have the old lady puppet lead the chant one more time. After the rhyme is finished, it is time for the old lady to depart as well.

Thank you for all your help, boys and girls. I'm tired after all this excitement, so I'm going in to take a nap.

Puppet yawns and stretches.

Good night, now.

Puppet goes slowly back into her bag.

Similar Story: Another successful story with a similar theme is the following tale, written for a slightly older audience:

Johnston, Tony. *The Soup Bone*. San Diego, CA: Harcourt Brace Jovanovich, 1990. **Ages:** 5 to 8. One Halloween night a lonely little old lady digs up a skeleton while digging for a good soup bone to beef up her thin soup. After some initial frights on both sides, the lady and the skeleton become friends and keep each other company. When they run out of things to do, the lady puts on her Halloween costume and joins the skeleton in scaring the townsfolk.

Share *The Soup Bone* and *The Little Old Lady Who Was Not Afraid of Anything* with 5 to 8 year olds. Then discuss the similarities and differences between the two stories with them.

NINE-IN-ONE, GRR! GRR!

Story Source: Blia Xiong. *Nine-in-One, Grr! Grr!: A Folktale from the Hmong People of Laos.* Illustrated by Nancy Hom. San Francisco: Children's Book Press, 1989.

Characters/Themes: Ecology, Jungle Beasts, Surprises

Ages: 6 to 8

Story Summary: A lonely tiger journeys to the sky to ask the great god Shao how many cubs she would have. When Shao, without thinking, answers nine a year, Tiger is very happy. Shao warns Tiger that she must remember his words because only then will the words come true. Tiger makes up a song to help her remember Shao's words.

Hearing the news, Bird realizes that nine cubs each year would produce way too many tigers. Bird cleverly tricks Tiger into reversing her song.

Children really appreciate Bird's clever trick, and sometimes they also enjoy joining you in singing Tiger's song as you present the story to them. The colorful illustrations by Nancy Hom are adapted from the Hmong technique of colorful multi-imaged embroidery. This book is always a favorite.

Puppet Needed: A tiger hand puppet is all that is needed to lead the discussion following this story.

Note: After you have some experience telling stories with puppets using scripts provided in this book, try learning this story to tell. It is very successfully told using just the tiger puppet, much like the hen acts her part and the storyteller plays all the other parts in the script for "The Little Red Hen and the Grain of Wheat." (See page 64.) You can also add a hand puppet bird and tell the story with the tiger and the bird using the same techniques presented in "The Gunny Wolf." (See page 69.)

Follow-up

Use Tiger to lead a discussion with the children about food chains. Use questions that cause the children to consider what would happen in the world if there were many more tigers. As the discussion progresses, have Tiger react as a tiger would to the children's answers. An example follows.

What to Say	What to Do
Storyteller: How did you like that story, Tiger?	Look into the bag, reach in, and put Tiger on your hand.
Tiger: I think that Bird tricked me!	Bring Tiger back out of her bag, grumbling.
Storyteller: Why do you think Bird would do such a thing?	Have Tiger look directly at the audience as you ask the question. You can call on someone or have Tiger call on someone to answer her.

Child: I think Bird tricked you because if you had nine cubs a year, soon there would be too many tigers.

Tiger: Too many tigers!

There can never be too many tigers in the world.

Tigers are fierce and brave and beautiful and strong.

The world can never have too many tigers.

Storyteller: Can anyone tell Tiger why it would be bad to have too many tigers?

Child: Well, Bird said if there were so many tigers they would eat everyone up.

Tiger: Wouldn't that be great!

Storyteller: Now wait just a minute, Tiger. How would you like it if there were nothing but tigers on the earth?

Tiger: That would be just fine. Then I wouldn't have to worry about any birds trying to trick me!

Storyteller: Boys and girls, what do you think would happen if the tigers ate up everyone else on the earth until only tigers were left?

Child: For one thing, they wouldn't have anything left to eat.

Storyteller: What would you think of that, Tiger?

Tiger: Wow, I guess Bird was right to trick me. Now I can see how too many tigers could be a bad thing, after all.

Tiger: If you happen to see Bird, tell him I'm not mad at him anymore for playing that trick on me. Now I understand why he did it. He just didn't want *too many* tigers on the earth.

She backs up to show her astonishment at that idea.

She speaks very firmly.

Now Tiger comes forward to convince her audience.

She shakes her head "no" as she speaks.

Tiger looks at you as you speak, then back toward the audience. Call on someone to answer your question.

Tiger looks toward the speaking child and nods "yes" vigorously.

She speaks enthusiastically.

Tiger looks back at you, and you look at Tiger as you ask her the question.

Tiger looks at you as she answers.

You and Tiger look toward the audience. Call on someone to answer.

Tiger jumps back with her mouth open in astonishment.

Tiger looks at you and then back at the audience.

Tiger looks at you and at the children as she answers.

After you have finished the discussion, Tiger cheerfully goes back into her bag.

Chapter Four
Leading Songs with Puppets

Puppets enhance songs in a number of ways. They focus the group's attention on the joy of singing. As with stories, they can introduce a song and/or lead follow-up activities and discussion. In addition, they can act out the song as it is being sung. Finally, and perhaps most importantly, they encourage audience participation. By doing any or all of these tasks they expand the audience's experience of the song.

This introduction provides general information on how to add puppetry to your songs. Following the introduction, five complete scripts for using puppets with specific songs are presented. The easier songs are listed first.

STEPS TO FOLLOW IN ADDING PUPPET ACTION TO A SONG

1. Choose a song you personally love as well as one you believe your audience will enjoy. If you love a song and enjoy singing it, your audience is more likely to love it, too.

2. Be very familiar with the song before adding puppet action.

3. Experiment with your puppet in front of a mirror. Allow yourself to be very playful, exploring what the puppet can appear to be doing as well as what it actually can do. For example, your puppet can tremble, and this movement can show excitement, anticipation, or fear, depending on the context. See Chapter 8 for more information on puppet movement.

4. If your puppet needs to appear to sing, practice this in front of the mirror. See Chapter 8 for tips on how to create the illusion your puppet is really singing.

5. Still using the mirror, practice adding puppet action to the song.

YOU CAN'T MAKE A TURTLE COME OUT*

Characters/Themes: Ecology, Turtles

Ages: 2 to 8

Most of the time your puppet will crawl or rest on your free arm. This picture illustrates the puppeteer using her free arm to gesture as she calls and coaxes the turtle to come out during the song.

Puppet Needed: You will need a turtle hand puppet that can draw his head in and out of his shell as well as walk around. Refer to Chapter 10 of this book for places to buy turtle puppets.

Voice: You will not need a voice for the turtle in this script.

Instructions: To prepare for this song, work with your turtle puppet in front of a mirror. Practice having him pull his head in and out of his shell. Try bringing it out very slowly and hesitantly. Then try pulling it in quickly, as if responding to a poke. Look at how the turtle looks walking along your free arm. Try having him rest against your body while you act out the verse that has you call him and coax him and shake him and *shout.* Work with the turtle until you can tell where the turtle's head is by how it feels on your hand without looking at it. During the song you will need to bring the turtle's head out and make him begin to walk around while you are not looking at him.

Listed on the next two pages are the words and music to the song. Sing the song aloud visualizing how a turtle puppet could be used to act out the words. Then refer to the script. The script gives specific instructions for ways you and your turtle puppet can bring the song to life. The script assumes the children know the song and can sing it with you. You can also present the song with the puppet as a new experience for the children, if you sing it by yourself.

Cassette Available: Malvina Reynolds sings "You Can't Make a Turtle Come Out" on her recording *Artichokes, Griddlecakes, and Other Good Things.* Order from: Sisters' Choice Recordings and Books, 1450 Sixth Street, Berkeley, CA 94710.

You Can't Make a Turtle Come Out

*words and music
by Malvina Reynolds*

If he wants to stay in his shell,
If he wants to stay in his shell,
You can knock on the door but you can't ring the bell,
And you can't make a turtle come out, come out,
You can't make a turtle come out.

Be kind to your four-footed friends,
Be kind to your four-footed friends,
A poke makes a turtle retreat at both ends,
And you can't make a turtle come out, come out,
You can't make a turtle come out.

So you'll have to patiently wait,
So you'll have to patiently wait,
And when he gets ready, he'll open the gate,
But you can't make a turtle come out, come out,
You can't make a turtle come out.

And when you forget that he's there,
And when you forget that he's there,
He'll be walking around with his head in the air,
But you can't make a turtle come out, come out,
You can't make a turtle come out.

Introduction

What to Say

Remember the song we've been singing all week about the turtle? Today I have a friend who is going to act out our song as we sing it. Wait a second and I'll bring out my turtle friend.

Let's sing our song, and maybe this shy turtle can help us.

What to Do

Reach into the bag by your side and put the turtle puppet on your hand, bringing it out slowly with its head withdrawn into its shell. The turtle rests on your free arm, which you are holding parallel to the floor. Look first at the turtle, then at the audience.

As you and the audience sing, you and the turtle act out the lyrics of the song.

The Song

Verse 1

You can't make a turtle come out,

You can't make a turtle come out.

You can call him

Or coax him

Or shake him

or *shout!*

But you can't make a turtle come out, come out,

You can't make a turtle come out.

Shake your head "no" slowly as you sing the first two lines.

Hold the turtle close to your body at the same level as when he was resting on your arm. Bring your free hand up, cup it around your mouth, and act as if you are calling the turtle as you and the audience sing.

Beckon the turtle with your free hand. The turtle still does not move.

Use your free hand to shake the turtle.

Shout this while looking from the turtle to the audience and back.

Shake your head "no." The turtle is resting on your free arm once more.

Verse 2

If he wants to stay in his shell,

If he wants to stay in his shell,

You can knock on the door

but you can't ring the bell,

And you can't make a turtle come out, come out,

You can't make a turtle come out.

Look at the audience and back at the turtle. The turtle does not move.

Knock on his shell with your free hand.

Use your free hand to pantomime ringing a bell near the turtle's concealed head.

Shake your head "no."

Verse 3

Be kind to your four-footed friends,

Be kind to your four-footed friends,

A poke makes a turtle retreat at both ends,

And you can't make a turtle come out, come out,

You can't make a turtle come out.

As you stroke the turtle's shell, he hesitantly peeks his head out for the first time.

Pretend to poke the shell, and the turtle pulls quickly back inside.

Shake your head "no."

Verse 4

So you'll have to patiently wait,

So you'll have to patiently wait,

And when he gets ready, he'll open the gate,

But you can't make a turtle come out, come out,

You can't make a turtle come out.

Sing softly and keep looking around but not at the turtle. The turtle's head comes farther and farther out of his shell.

Shake your head "no."

Verse 5

And when you forget that he's there,

And when you forget that he's there,
He'll be walking around with his head in the air,

But you can't make a turtle come out, come out,

You can't make a turtle come out.

Now the turtle's head is completely out and he's stretching his neck out as he begins to walk along your free arm. As he does, look at him with great astonishment and delight.

Shake your head "no" just as seriously as you did before.

Follow-up

Storyteller: Children, thank you for helping to sing that song. And turtle, thank you for showing us what you like and what you don't like.

Turtle, resting on your free arm, looks up at you and nods his head "yes."

Turtle, would you stay out here for a little while longer and help us?

Turtle nods again, and you turn to the audience.

Children, raise your hand if you can tell Turtle and me something from the song about what Turtle likes or doesn't like.

A sample interaction follows, suggesting a way of leading the discussion with the turtle puppet.

Kathy, thank you for raising your hand. What did you learn about Turtle's likes and dislikes?

Turtle looks at Kathy as she speaks.

Kathy: I think he likes it when we leave him alone. He doesn't like it when you poke him.

Turtle slowly nods that she is right.

Storyteller: Turtle says you're right Kathy. He does not like to be poked. Ben, did you have an idea?	**Turtle looks at Ben as he speaks.**
Ben: He doesn't like it if we *shout!*	**Turtle quickly pulls his head back into his shell.**
Storyteller: Well we can see that you're right, Ben. Turtle didn't like it at all when you shouted. Now he's back into his shell. Does anyone have an idea what we could do to get him to come again.	**This discussion can continue as long as it seems productive, using Turtle's actions to reinforce the information presented in the song. When you have finished the discussion, thank the turtle and gently place him back in his bag.**

THE BEAR WENT OVER THE MOUNTAIN

Characters/Theme: Bears, Humor

Ages: 2 to 7

Puppet Needed: You will need one bear hand puppet. This song can be done with any bear hand puppet, whether or not its mouth moves. In this script, the bear's name is Bobbie. You may call your bear whatever you like.

Instructions: The song may be performed in two different ways. The way that is described in detail here involves using your body as the mountain, with Bobbie acting out the song as you and the children sing it.

Another activity to do with this song is to have one child or several children from the audience volunteer to come up to the front, using their bodies to make the mountain that Bobbie the Bear then climbs.

As you begin to prepare this activity, practice climbing motions with your puppet while watching in a mirror to see what is especially effective. Try having her rock back and forth as she moves forward. She may have trouble in spots and slip back down a little before catching herself through grabbing your arm in her mouth or with her front feet. Experiment and play with your puppet to find what works best for you. Practice climbing down as well as up your free arm and shoulder. It will probably be necessary for the bear to back down. That's fine. If you and Bobbie act like this is normal, the children won't mind either. (Besides, it is the best way to climb down anyway.)

Introduction

What to Say

Bobbie, remember that song we've been practicing?

Well, look at all these boys and girls who are here to help us sing it.

What to Do

Bring out the bag with Bobbie the Bear inside. Begin by looking in and putting your hand into the bag so you can put on the puppet. Bobbie pops her head out of the bag and nods vigorously, looking at you.

You and Bobbie both turn to look at the audience. Bobbie reacts with astonishment, opening her mouth wide (if she has a mouth that opens) and quickly backing up.

Isn't that great?

Look back to Bobbie, who again enthusiastically nods her head "yes!"

Come on out so we can begin.

Bobbie climbs all the way out of the bag, and you put the bag down on the floor. Bobbie sits on your free arm, which you are holding in front of your body with your elbow bent. As you and the children begin singing the song, Bobbie acts it out in pantomime. Divide your attention, alternating between watching Bobbie climb and looking at the children to encourage them to sing with you.

The Song

The bear went over the mountain.
The bear went over the mountain.

Bobbie slowly climbs up your left arm and shoulder, using whatever climbing motions you hage already discovered work best for the way the bear is made.

The bear went over the moun . . . taainnnn

To see what she could see.

Bobbie should make it to the top of your shoulder as you sing this line.

And all that she could see . . .

Bobbie looks behind you over your shoulder and back toward the audience several times.

And all that she could seeeee.

Waaaasss . . .

The other side of the mountain,

Bobbie stays at the top of your shoulder but turns to the audience and sings with you! You sing in a lower, bear-like voice and move Bobbie to show she is singing. If she has a moving mouth, move that as she sings. If her mouth does not move, tilt her head back and forth in time with the music. She may use her front paws to clap along in time with the music if that is comfortable. Refer to Chapter Eight for help with puppet voice and movement.

The other side of the mountain,

The other side of the moun . . . taainnnn,

Was all that she did see.

So the bear went down the mountain,
The bear went down the mountain,
The bear went down the moun . . . taainnnn,
Naturally.

Bobbie no longer sings but resumes acting out the song in pantomime as you sing the remainder. By the end of the song, she has climbed back down to sit on your free arm as she was at the beginning of the song.

Conclusion

Thanks, Bobbie, for acting out that song for us.

Bobbie takes a bow and then looks at you.

And thanks to all of you for helping us sing that song.

You and Bobbie turn to the audience, and Bobbie nods "yes."

Bye for now, Bobbie.

Bobbie waves a paw or says good-bye to the children and climbs back into her bag.

It looks like Bobbie will be taking a nap in her bag while we go on to the next story, children. Sleep tight, Bobbie.

Peek inside the bag for just a second, then put the bag away.

Max the Monster dances with delight during the Peanut Butter/Jelly! song. Note how the puppeteer's free hand gives Max a place to stand and dance.

PEANUT BUTTER/JELLY!

Themes: Food, Humor

Ages: All ages. This song delights everyone, from preschoolers to grandparents. My puppet even had a sophisticated sixth-grade class writing new peanut butter and jelly songs for him after they saw this song performed.

Puppet Needed: I use a friendly, furry monster hand puppet named Max. Of course, you can use another name for your puppet if you prefer. Mine has a moving mouth and arms and legs that swing freely as I move the puppet.

If you do not have a monster puppet, experiment with other puppets you already own or puppets you are considering purchasing to see which one moves in ways that enhance the action of this song. Use a puppet with a moving mouth if possible. I find that arms and legs that swing freely also really enhance the action of the song.

Prop Needed: I use a fake peanut butter and jelly sandwich as a prop to entice Max back into his bag at the end of the song. You can make a sandwich prop from two slices of ½" polyfoam for the bread. Shape the slices appropriately and color the "crust" with a permanent brown felt marker. The sandwich filling can be represented by a piece of purple felt for the jelly and brown felt for the peanut butter. Put your sandwich in a sandwich bag that has a plastic zipper-type lock and all the parts will stay together. The children know immediately that it is a peanut butter and jelly sandwich. If you do not wish to make a sandwich, you can use a paperback book of his "favorite" story or other treat to entice him to go back into his bag.

Instructions: Rehearse in front of a mirror, trying out different ways the puppet can add action to this song. Practice showing the puppet dancing; picking peanuts and grapes; smashing, spreading, biting, chewing, and swallowing; being shy; and whispering in your ear.

Sing or chant the song first without the puppet, visualizing all the ways a puppet could add action to the song. After you learn the words, practice singing or chanting the song with your puppet performing the actions indicated.

The complete text of the song is listed next so you may read through it easily, visualizing ways a puppet might enhance the song through action.

Following the complete text of the song is the script, which lists the ways Max acts out the song.

The Peanut Butter/Jelly! Song

The song may be sung or chanted rhythmically. Feel free to make up a tune that is comfortable for you if you choose to sing the song. The word *jelly* is always done in a loud whisper.

Chorus

Peanut, peanut butter . . . jelly!
Peanut, peanut butter . . . jelly!

Verse 1

First you take the peanuts and you pick 'em, you pick 'em,
You pick 'em, pick 'em, pick 'em.
Then you smash 'em, you smash 'em,
You smash 'em, smash 'em, smash 'em.
Then you spread 'em, you spread 'em,
You spread 'em, spread 'em, spread 'em.
Singin' . . .

[Repeat Chorus]

Verse 2

Then you take the grapes and you pick 'em, you pick 'em,
You pick 'em, pick 'em, pick 'em.
Then you smash 'em, you smash 'em,
You smash 'em, smash 'em, smash 'em.
Then you spread 'em, you spread 'em,
You spread 'em, spread 'em, spread 'em.
Singin' . . .

[Repeat Chorus]

Verse 3

Then you take the bread and you spread it, you spread it,
You spread it, spread it, spread it.
Then you smash it, you smash it,
You smash it, smash it, smash it.
Then you bite, you bite,
You bite, bite, bite.
Then you chew, you chew,
You chew, chew, chew.
Then you swallow, you swallow,
You swallow, swallow, swallow.
Singin' . . .

[Repeat Chorus]

(Sing the final chorus sounding muffled, as if your mouth was still full of . . . peanut butter and jelly!)

The Script: The Peanut Butter/Jelly! Song

Each time you sing the chorus Max dances around, always opening his mouth to loudly whisper *jelly!* with the rest of you. When you sing the verses, Max acts them out.

Chorus

> Peanut, peanut butter . . . jelly!
> Peanut, peanut butter . . . jelly!

Introduction

What to Say

When I found out I was coming to visit you, I told my good friend Max. He said he'd like to come, too. Max lives in this bag.

Now there is one thing about Max. He really likes to sleep in the mornings. In fact, he prefers to wake up around 1:30 in the afternoon.

This is going to be really hard for him to get up so early. He said that he really wanted to meet you all, so I'll try to wake him up.

So you can imagine that this is his favorite time to come out and meet people. He was really glad to hear that I was coming here at (whatever time it is).

Max, are you awake in there?

Hello, Max, we're here at (name the school, library, or event). Remember I told you I was coming, and you said you wanted to come, too? Well, it's time to come out and meet everybody.

Max, aren't you coming out?

You're not coming out?

But Max, everyone is waiting to meet you. So you have to come out. You don't have to stay out if you don't want to, but you have to come out and meet everyone.

What to Do

Pick up the shopping bag from the inconspicuous spot where you placed it earlier.

Look at your watch.

Say this if the performance is before 1:30 in the afternoon.

Say this if the performance is at or after 1:30 in the afternoon.

With one hand, hold the side or the handle of the bag while you put your other hand inside the bag to "wake him up" (and, also, to put him on). As you speak to Max, look into the bag at him. Throughout the rest of this activity, appear to divide your attention between the audience and Max.

Look in the bag and speak to Max.

Silent pause. Look at the audience and then back into the bag.

Using your hand that is inside the puppet in the bag, swish the puppet against the sides of the bag to make it rattle loudly, as if Max is inside shaking his head "NO!"

More bag rattling. Look at audience in surprise, then back into the bag at Max.

Come on, Max. Hurry up.

Max? Max! Come out!

I know you'll like these people.

So, Max, don't these people look like fun?

Max, are you afraid of that person?

Ever so slowly, parts of Max begin to appear out of the top of the bag. Alternate among speaking encouragingly to him, urging him to hurry up, and reassuring him. Last of all, his eyes peek over the top of the bag. He timidly looks around at everyone as you speak.

Just then, Max looks right at one child. Be careful to pick a child who does not look the least bit hesitant or frightened of the puppet. Max opens his mouth wide and hops quickly back into the bag!

A variation is to directly ask the child if he or she made a mean face at Max.

Worried about meeting new people, Max the Monster is reluctant to come out of his bag.

She (or he) looks very nice to me. She's smiling right now. Come out and take a look.

Max peeks out at the child, nods his head in agreement that she is indeed smiling, jumps out of the bag, and hides his head on your shoulder. Put the bag down at your feet or on a nearby table and begin petting the back of Max's head with your free hand.

You know, Max, it's nice that you came out of the bag, but they don't want to see your back. They want to see your face. Turn around.

Max, trembling, shakes his head "no" with his face still hidden against your shoulder.

Well, boys and girls, when Max first meets people sometimes he feels kind of shy. Maybe if he knows that you like something he likes, he'll feel better. Raise your hand if you really and truly like peanut butter and jelly sandwiches.

Turn to the audience now, still petting Max with your free hand. As hands go into the air, tap Max on the back with your free hand to get his attention.

Max, turn around and look how many people here like peanut butter and jelly sandwiches. Isn't that amazing?

Max turns to look over the people with their hands in the air, growing more and more excited as he looks around the room. He shows his excitement by opening his mouth wider and wider as he sees more hands in the air.

39

Now, Max, are you going to stay out here and talk with us?

Max looks at you and his head and shoulders droop as he turns to hide his head on your shoulder again. Speak to the audience.

Well, you can put your hands down now. There is one thing we can do that is guaranteed to get Max to turn around. We can sing the "Peanut Butter/Jelly!" song. Would you like that, Max?

As you look down at Max he nods "yes" without looking at the audience. Then you look back at the children.

Now don't worry if you don't know the song. It's really easy to learn. In fact, the chorus has only three words in it, and I'll bet some of you can guess what they are.

Children may call out the answer. If they don't, call on someone who has a hand raised, or just tell the answer.

You're right, peanut . . . butter . . . jelly! And this is how it goes.

Begin by singing just the chorus over and over. Usually, the children join in almost immediately. If they are hesitant, invite them to sing with you. At first, Max still has his face against your shoulder. Then his head and body start to move, keeping time with the music. After you sing the lines two or three times, Max begins to whip his head around to look at the children, whisper "jelly" with them, and hide his face again. After a few more times, Max finally is facing the children and dancing as they sing the chorus. Suddenly Max stops and lies down on your arm.

Wait, let's stop singing while I ask Max something. Max, why did you quit dancing?

Max looks up at you as you ask the question, then whispers in your ear.

Oh, so you want to sing the entire "Peanut Butter/Jelly!" song.

Max nods his head enthusiastically, looking first at you and then at the children.

We can do that. Get ready, Max.

Max stands up again on your free hand, and you tell the children how they will sing the song.

Twice we'll sing the part we've just been singing, and then we'll sing a verse. Are you ready, Max?

Max looks himself up and down, then looks at you and nods.

Do you think they're ready?

Use your free hand to point to the audience. Max looks at the audience very carefully, then looks at you and nods again.

All right. Here we go!

The Song

What to Sing or Chant Is in *Italics*; What to Say Is Not

What to Do

Verse 1

First you take the peanuts and you pick 'em, you pick 'em,

Max pretends to pick with his mouth.

You pick 'em, pick 'em, pick 'em.

Then you smash 'em, you smash 'em,

Max smashes 'em on your free arm, which you hold in front of you with your elbow bent and your forearm parallel to the floor.

You smash 'em, smash 'em, smash 'em.	
Then you spread 'em, you spread 'em,	**Max spreads them by sitting on your free arm and waving his hands and arms through the air.**
You spread 'em, spread 'em, spread 'em.	
Singin'. . .	
[Chorus]	**Max dances with delight.**

Verse 2

Then you take the grapes and you pick 'em, you pick 'em,	**Acted out with the same movements Max used in Verse 1.**
You pick 'em, pick 'em, pick 'em.	**Here Max stops dancing and looks at you. You stop singing, so the children stop, too. If they don't stop, tell them to stop so you can talk to Max.**
Max, what is wrong?	**Look at Max. He whispers into your ear.**
Good idea, Max.	**He nods "yes."**
Max says we do the same thing to the grapes we just did to the peanuts, so you can all sing it with us.	**You and Max both look at the children. Max nods "yes" again, slowly and emphatically.**
Then you take the grapes and you pick 'em, you pick 'em,	**You and Max begin the second verse again, encouraging the children to sing with you as Max acts it out.**
You pick 'em, pick 'em, pick 'em.	
Then you smash 'em, you smash 'em,	
You smash 'em, smash 'em, smash 'em.	
Then you spread 'em, you spread 'em,	
You spread 'em, spread 'em, spread 'em.	
Singin'. . .	
[Chorus]	**Again, Max dances with delight.**

Verse 3

Then you take the bread and you spread it, you spread it,	**Max sits on your free arm and waves his arms in a spreading motion.**
You spread it, spread it, spread it.	
Then you smash it, you smash it,	**Max jumps up and down with smashing motions on your arm. At this point, you may wish to stop him with the following routine.**
Max, stop!	**Max stops and looks at you.**
Are you telling me that you smash your sandwiches *before* you eat them?	**Sound as if you cannot believe what you are saying. Max looks at you and then at the children and nods his head just a tiny bit.**
But, Max, that's not civilized!	**He leans back, looking at you and opening his mouth in astonishment.**

No one here smashes their sandwiches before they eat them.

You and Max look at the audience. Almost always at least one child shouts "I do!" Usually many children say that they do. If that is so, you react with surprise at all the sandwich smashers in the crowd. If no children say they smash their sandwiches, then Max whispers in your ear that he's going to teach the children the monster way to eat a sandwich, and you tell the children what he said before continuing.

OK, Max, we'll do it your way.

Nod "yes" to Max and look with amused resignation at the children.

Then you take the bread and you spread it, you spread it,

Max sits on your arm and waves his arms in a spreading motion.

You spread it, spread it, spread it.

Then youuuuuuuuuuuuuu

Long pause as Max stands on your arm and pumps his knees and moves up and down, winding up for a spectacular smash.

Smash it, you smash it,

Wildly, Max jumps up and down on your arm, his landings timed to coincide with each time you sing the word "smash."

You smash it, smash it, smash it.

Then you bite, you bite,

Max makes biting motions with his mouth each time you sing the word "bite".

You bite, bite, bite.

Then you chew, you chew,

Max chews through this part, looking around at the kids.

You chew, chew, chew.

Then you swallow, you swallow,

Max swallows five times, once for each time you say the word. You may wish to accompany each swallow with a "gulp" sound.

You swallow, swallow, swallow.

Singin'. . .

[Chorus]

This last time, sing the chorus muffled, as if your mouth was still full of peanut butter and jelly! As the chorus dies away, Max settles into your lap and begins to suck his thumb, looking contentedly at the audience.

Conclusion

Max, aren't you glad you came out to meet these people?

Max looks up at you and nods.

But now it's time to go back into your bag.

Pick up the bag. Max looks in but quickly pops back out.

Don't you want to go?

Max shakes his head "no."

Well, it's time for your lunch. Let me show you what I made for you this morning.

Reach into the bag and pull out the foam and felt peanut butter and jelly sandwich. Max looks at the audience, showing his delight with a wide open mouth, then quickly grabs the sandwich out of your hand and holds it in his mouth. He drops the sandwich in the bag, and then looks back at the children.

I think Max likes you better than a peanut butter and jelly sandwich!

Max nods "yes."

That means he really likes you a lot!!

Max nods "yes" even more enthusiastically.

I know you like them, Max, but it's time for us to go on to the next story. So go on into your bag, Max. If you eat quietly, you can listen to the stories from inside your bag.

With one last look at the audience, Max reluctantly hops back into his bag, still holding the sandwich in his mouth. Look into the bag and reach in to help him get settled.

Get comfy in there, Max, and try not to get peanut butter everywhere. Good-bye, Max!

I KNOW AN OLD LADY WHO SWALLOWED A FLY

Themes: Food, Humor, Imagination

Ages: All ages

Puppets Needed: You will need one hand puppet with a large moving mouth. If you have an old woman puppet, you will not need to do any special costuming. If you do not have an old woman, try using an animal puppet with a large, expressive moving mouth. An alligator is a fun animal to try. The use of an animal to play the part of the old woman can add even more humor to the song. You may wish to put a scarf on your animal or use some other costume idea to show that she is an old woman.

You will need to make simple figures for all the creatures the old woman swallows, except the fly—spider, bird, cat, dog, goat, cow, and horse. Each one must be slightly bigger than the one before, with the cow and horse being noticeably bigger than the others. Durable creatures can be made of 1/2-inch polyfoam. Decorate the foam by coloring it with permanent felt markers. White or cream-colored foam can sometimes be purchased at upholstery shops, surplus stores, carpet stores, and fabric stores, as well as foam stores. Flat foam puppets are easily seen by the audience and can be convincingly chewed on by the old woman without damage to the puppet.

If necessary, you may use cardboard instead of foam to make the creatures. The cardboard figures will still be easily seen by the audience, but they will not last through many performances of the song.

You will also need a box or bag large enough to store these puppets and also big enough so that the old lady can thrust her head down into the box or bag, out of sight of the audience. In the instructions and script, I will refer to this as a bag, but a proper size box will also work.

Instructions: Many people who think of performing this song can only imagine how to do it in a literal manner. In other words, they think the old lady puppet must actually swallow the creatures.

Simple, childlike drawings work well for making all the creatures the old woman swallows. Inspiration for these drawings provided by Pam Wade.

This script presents an equally effective and much simpler way to act out this delightful song. All the creatures the old lady will eat are given to children in the audience before the song begins. Depending on the space in the room and how the children are reacting, you can have all the children with creatures come up and sit in the front row before the song begins, or you can carry the old lady through the audience looking for the things she wants to eat as the song progresses.

When the old lady takes a creature from the child who is holding it, she can chew on the creature and dance around as you and the audience continue the song. Eventually, the old lady returns to the large bag in which she lives, plunging her head in out of sight of the audience with the creature still in her mouth. The old lady does all of her serious eating inside this bag. Therefore, the audience imagines her swallowing all the creatures. Actually, she just drops the creatures in the bag and reappears, still chewing and swallowing.

Practice in front of a mirror the movements the old lady must do. Make sure she can easily grasp the creatures in her mouth. Look at ways of making her appear to chew and swallow. Devote some practice time to her dancing moves, as she will be dancing a great deal as you and the children sing the song, and you need to have lots of variety in the ways she can move. As she dances, try using your other arm as her stage. Look at how she looks moving through the air, keeping a consistent height to create the illusion that she is dancing on the ground.

Remember, at the end of the song, the old lady dies. Read the conclusion in the script, and practice the actions called for in front of a mirror.

Introduction

What to Say

Girls and boys, today we are going to use puppets to help us sing a song. I'm going to show you some of the creatures in the song, and I'll bet you can guess the name of the song we will be singing.

There is a horse, a cow, a spider, a dog, a bird, a goat, and a cat.

What to Do

As you speak, reach for the bag in which the old lady and her creatures are kept. Set the bag down in a place that is easy for you to reach but higher than the children. If the children are sitting on the floor, put the bag on a chair or high stool. This will prevent curious children from sneaking up to peek in the bag during the song.

Hold up the creatures, not in the order the old lady will be eating them, and invite the children to name them with you.

Can you guess the name of the song?

Children may guess "Old MacDonald" as well as the correct song title. If they do not guess soon, tell them the song title and move on.

That's right! We're singing "I Know an Old Lady Who Swallowed a Fly." I need some of you to hold these creatures until it's time for the old lady to

swallow them.

Hold the creatures up one at a time, ask the children to make sounds like that creature, and then hand the creature to someone in the audience. Do this quickly and decisively so children do not

have time to be very disappointed at not being chosen. Be certain to choose older, confident-looking children to hold the goat and the cow.

Now I need everyone's help. What is the first thing the old lady eats?

Emphasize how *everyone* is helping now to encourage those children not chosen to hold a puppet. Children will answer with "a fly!"

Yes, a fly. Now, please make the sound of a fly to call the old lady out of her bag. Buzzzzzzzzzzzzzz.

Make the buzzing sound with the children to encourage them. As you all buzz, have the old lady puppet slowly climb out of her bag and sit on your arm.

Old lady, do you hear that fly? Look around. See if you can find it.

Have the old lady look all around the room, as if searching for the fly.

There it is! You've got it, old lady!

Finally, have her focus on one spot, open her mouth, grab the imaginary fly, chew for a moment, and then swallow. The minute she bites the fly, stop making the buzzing sounds, and the children will stop, too. If they do not stop, tell them they don't need to buzz anymore because the old lady has found her fly. Begin the song as the old lady swallows the fly.

The Song

What to Sing Is in Italics; What to Say Is Not

What to Do

Verse 1

I know an old lady who swallowed a fly.

Throughout the song, you alternate between watching the old lady and looking at the audience. The old lady also alternates between looking at you and at the audience.

I don't know why she swallowed the fly.

The old lady shakes her head "no" and puts her head down sadly for just a moment.

Perhaps she'll die.

Verse 2

I know an old lady who swallowed a spider . . .

The old lady looks up in a perky manner, and she begins looking around the room for the spider. When she finds it, she takes it in her mouth and goes back into her bag for a moment. Out of sight, she drops the spider into the bag.

45

She hates for anyone to see her eat, so she always eats in her bag.	Say this as an aside to the audience, while the old lady has her head out of sight in the bag.
That wiggled and jiggled and tickled inside her.	She brings her head out of the bag, swallows, and begins laughing and jiggling.
She swallowed the spider to catch the fly.	As you sing this part, the old lady dances around, ending up a bit sad-looking on the last line.
But I don't know why she swallowed the fly. *Perhaps she'll die.*	

Verse 3

I know an old lady who swallowed a bird.	The old lady looks around with interest.
Can you make the sound of a bird to help her find it?	As you and the children make bird sounds, the old lady finds the bird and takes it into her mouth. The bird sounds stop.
How absurd, to swallow a bird.	You sound astonished as you sing. The old lady looks at the audience, with the bird hanging out of her mouth.
She swallowed the bird to catch the spider	She puts her head into the bag to "eat," dropping the bird out of sight and coming out of the bag chewing and swallowing.
That wiggled and jiggled and tickled inside her.	You sing this line with a giggle in your voice as she wiggles and jiggles.
She swallowed the spider to catch the fly. *But I don't know why she swallowed the fly.*	She dances as you sing these lines, ending up looking a bit sad on the last line.
Perhaps she'll die.	

Verse 4

I know an old lady who swallowed a . . .	
What comes next?	You and the old lady look at the children, who answer, "cat."
That's right. Do you see a cat around here, old lady?	She looks at you as you ask her the question; then she looks around the room for the cat. When she sees it, she goes over and takes the cat in her mouth.
Fancy that, to swallow a cat.	She turns to the audience so they see the cat in her mouth before going into her bag to eat (and to drop the cat out of sight).
She swallowed the cat to catch the bird.	She comes up swallowing and nods "yes."
She swallowed the bird to catch the spider that wiggled and jiggled and tickled inside her.	She wiggles and jiggles.
She swallowed the spider to catch the fly.	She dances around, looking sad again on the last line.
But I don't know why she swallowed the fly. *Perhaps she'll die.*	

Verse 5

I know an old lady who swallowed a . . .

The old lady begins looking around. Have her go over to the goat.

Is this the next animal?

Point to the goat as you ask the children. The children will answer, "No, the dog comes next."

The children say the dog comes next.

Look at the old lady as you speak.

See if you can find the dog, old lady.

The old lady nods "yes" and begins to look around.

Children, let's make the sound of a dog to help her find it. Rrruf, rufff, rrrrruf!

As you and the children bark, the old lady finds the dog and takes it into her mouth. The barking stops.

What a hog, to swallow a dog!

You sound a bit disgusted on this line. The old lady looks at the audience with the dog in her mouth, goes into her bag for a minute, and then comes out chewing and swallowing.

She swallowed the dog to catch the cat.

She nods her head "yes" and begins to dance.

She swallowed the cat to catch the bird.

She swallowed the bird to catch the spider that wiggled and jiggled and tickled inside her.

She wiggles and jiggles, looking at the audience and down at her stomach.

She swallowed the spider to catch the fly.

She dances, looking sad at the last line.

But I don't know why she swallowed the fly.

Perhaps she'll die.

Verse 6

I know an old lady who swallowed a . . .

Look at the audience, inviting them to say the animal by your pause in the singing and by your look. The old lady begins to look around the room.

GOAT!

After your pause, finish the line whether the children have helped or not.

She just opened her throat . . .

The old lady goes over to the child with the goat, turns on her back, and opens her mouth as wide as it will go.

And in walked the goat.

Invite the child to walk the goat into the old lady's mouth. The old lady closes her mouth on the goat, stands up facing the audience with the goat hanging out of her mouth, and then goes into her bag to "eat."

She swallowed the goat to catch the dog.

She comes up chewing, swallows, and begins to dance.

She swallowed the dog to catch the cat.

She nods her head "yes" while continuing to dance.

She swallowed the cat to catch the bird.

She swallowed the bird to catch the spider that wiggled and jiggled and tickled inside her.

She wiggles and jiggles, looking at the audience and down at her stomach.

She swallowed the spider to catch the fly.

She dances, looking sad at the last line.

But I don't know why she swallowed the fly.

Perhaps she'll die.

Verse 7

I know an old lady who swallowed a . . .	Pause for the children to fill in the animal. The old lady begins to look around.
cow!	Say "cow" with astonishment. The old lady sees the cow, turns around, and starts hurrying away from it.
Old lady, where are you going? The cow is behind you.	The old lady whispers something in your ear, and once again turns away from the cow.
Girls and boys, the old lady says that cow is too big and she is *not* eating it.	Look at the children with surprise as you say this line.
Old lady, if you do not eat this cow, we cannot finish the song.	Stop the old lady with your free hand and speak to her earnestly. She firmly shakes her head "no" and continues walking away from the cow.
Children, do you think she can eat this cow?	As you turn to the children, the old lady stops walking and turns to look at the children as they reply. Almost always, the children reply with an enthusiastic "yes!" If they seem uncertain, encourage them just as you encourage the old lady, because the cow *has* to be eaten to finish the song.
You can do it, old lady. Get ready.	The old lady puffs up her chest and looks at the cow with determination.
Come on, old lady, go for it!	She goes to the cow, takes it in her mouth, and turns to the audience.
Wow, that is a really big cow. But I know you can do it, old lady.	She goes into her bag, comes up chewing, and goes back in for more bites.
Keep working at it, old lady.	Look into the bag to check on her progress as she comes up chewing and goes back in several times.
Finally . . . *you did it!*	Speak with triumph as the old lady slowly comes out of the bag and swallows one last time.
Are you feeling pretty full now, old lady?	She nods "yes."
Well, there is just one animal left, and then you will have finished the song. I know you can do it, for show business!	The old lady perks up and begins looking around for the final animal.

Verse 8

I know an old lady who swallowed a . . . horse . . .	Pause so the children can say "horse" with you. The old lady takes the horse, goes into her bag, and comes out chewing and swallowing. Don't sing the last line until the old lady is back out of her bag.
She died, of course.	Say this in a matter-of-fact tone as the old lady keels over to lie, face up, cradled in your free arm. Look at the children in surprise and then back down at the old lady with concern.

Conclusion

Old lady, are you really dead?	Pause for a moment, then move some part of the old lady. Begin with very slight movements. Move her mouth a little, turn her head very slightly, and begin to move her chest up and down as if she is breathing.
Children, do you think she's really dead?	Look at the children and then back to the old lady, who is moving a little more now.
Old lady, I think you are all right.	She lifts her head to look up at you, nodding "yes."
Get up and take a bow, old lady!	She stands up and bows to the children.
Boys and girls, let's give the old lady a big hand for being so brave and for eating all those animals so we could finish our song.	Old lady continues to bow, first to one side of the audience and then the other, as the children clap.
After all that work, old lady, you deserve a rest. Here, let me help you into your bag where you can take a nice long nap.	Old lady walks back and climbs into her bag, and you leave her there.
And thank you, too, girls and boys, for all your help in singing "I Know an Old Lady Who Swallowed a Fly."	

THE BOY AND THE BEAR*

Characters/Themes: Bears, Ecology, Friends, Surprises

Ages: 4 to 8. Do this song at a quiet time when the children are ready and able to listen with their hearts. This song is good preparation for a quiet activity, such as silent reading or napping.

Puppet Needed: A bear puppet with a moving mouth is best. The song can also be done with a bear puppet without a moving mouth; this puppet will have to move her head and body in time with the music to show when she is singing.

Voices: You will need three different-sounding voices for this song: the bear, the boy, and your own voice acting as narrator. Try using a lower, very earnest tone for the bear. The little boy's voice will be different if you make him sound young and innocent, with a slightly higher voice than your natural tone. Use your own comfortable voice for the narrator in the song.

*Words and music by Bonnie Lockhart.

Instructions: Play with the bear puppet in front of a mirror. Have her sit comfortably on your free forearm or on the arm of your chair. She must be able to look back and forth from you to the audience, move her mouth or her body to create the illusion that she is actually singing her part, and yawn, stretch, and go to sleep on your shoulder or in the crook of your arm.

Be comfortable with the words and tune before you add the bear's movements to your song. Sing the entire song aloud two or three times, experimenting with changing your voice for the three characters. To keep the rhythm of the song, you will need to leave in the words that explain who is singing. Sing those in the narrator's voice. Sing only the actual words that the boy and the bear sing in their voices.

Listed on the next two pages are the words and music to the song. After you are comfortable singing it using the tips about voices included here, read the script and practice adding the bear's actions to the song. Give special attention to creating the illusion that the bear is really singing during her singing parts. See Chapter 8 if you need help with the voices.

Cassette Available: "The Boy and the Bear" is sung by Bonnie Lockhart on the cassette tape *Dinosaur and Other Songs from the Plum City Players*. Order from: Sister's Choice Recordings and Books, 1450 Sixth Street, Berkeley, CA 94710.

Introduction:

What to Sing Is in *Italics*; What to Say Is Not | **What to Do**

Girls and boys, I'm going to sing a song for you, with help from a friend of mine. This song tells a story.

Pick up the bag containing the bear that you have already placed nearby.

Bear, are you ready to come out? Come on, all the boys and girls are waiting to see you and to hear your song.

Look into the bag. Then reach in to put the bear on your hand as you encourage her.

I'm glad you could come and share your song with us. . . . Let's begin!

Bring the bear out to sit on your free arm or the arm of the chair. Look at the bear as you speak. The bear looks at you and then nods "yes."

The Song

Verse 1

A boy and a bear were the best of friends,

Both you and the bear look toward the audience.

And they played in the forest where the river bends,

And the bear really wanted to teach that kid

You look at the bear, who nods "yes," and you both look back at the audience.

Some special bear things that she did.

THE BOY AND THE BEAR

by Bonnie Lockhart

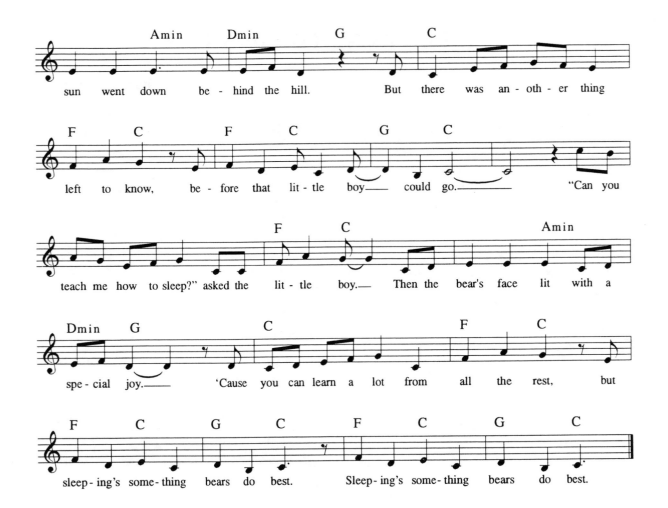

3. "Can you teach me how to hop?" asked the little guy
"Oh no," said the bear, "But we can try
To find the rabbit, 'cause that's his habit;
We'll find the rabbit, 'cause that's his habit."

4. "Can you teach me how to build?" asked the little guy
"Oh no, " said the bear, "But we can try
To find the beaver, she's very clever;
We'll find the beaver, she's very clever."

5. "Can you teach me how to sing?" asked the little guy
"Oh no," said the bear, "But we can try
To find the cricket, he's in the thicket;
We'll find the cricket, he's in the thicket."

The Boy And The Bear - page 2

Verse 2

"Can you teach me how to fly?" asked the little guy.

"Oh no," said the bear, "but we can try

To find the bat, she's good at that,

We'll find the bat, she's good at that."

Use the little boy voice you've practiced, and look at the bear, as if you are the little boy singing the question to her. Looking at you, the bear shakes her head "no" as she sings the beginning of her answer. As she sings the rest, she looks around the audience as if looking for the bat.

Verse 3

"Can you teach me how to hop?" asked the little guy.

"Oh no," said the bear, "but we can try

To find the rabbit, 'cause that's his habit;

We'll find the rabbit, 'cause that's his habit."

Use the little boy voice you've practiced, and look at the bear, as if you are the little boy singing the question to her. Looking at you, the bear shakes her head "no" as she sings the beginning of her answer. As she sings the rest, she looks around the audience as if looking for the rabbit.

Verse 4

"Can you teach me how to build?" asked the little guy.

"Oh no," said the bear, "but we can try

To find the beaver, she's very clever;

We'll find the beaver, she's very clever."

Use the little boy voice you've practiced, and look at the bear, as if you are the little boy singing the question to her. Looking at you, the bear shakes her head "no" as she sings the beginning of her answer. As she sings the rest, she looks around the audience as if looking for the beaver.

Verse 5

"Can you teach me how to sing?" asked the little guy.

"Oh no," said the bear, "but we can try

To find the cricket, he's in the thicket;

We'll find the cricket, he's in the thicket."

Use the little boy voice you've practiced, and look at the bear, as if you are the little boy singing the question to her. Looking at you, the bear shakes her head "no" as she sings the beginning of her answer. As she sings the rest, she looks around the audience as if looking for the cricket.

Verse 6

So all of the animals shared their skill,

And the sun went down behind the hill.

But there was another thing left to know,

Before that little boy could go.

You and the bear look out at the audience, moving slightly in time with the music.

Verse 7

"Can you teach me how to sleep?" asked the little boy.

Use the little boy voice you've practiced, and look at the bear, as if you are the little boy singing the question to her.

Then the bear's face lit with a special joy.

'Cause you can learn a lot from all the rest,

but sleeping's something bears do best.

Sleeping's something bears do best.

The bear shows pure delight by slowly opening her arms and her mouth wide and looking around at the children. Then the bear yawns, stretches, and snuggles down into the crook of your elbow with her head facing away from the audience. Sing the last line of the song slowly and gently. As the song ends, the bear snores softly.

Conclusion

Well, it looks as if our bear is sound asleep. I'll put her into her bag where she can have a comfortable nap. You go quietly to your next activity, so you won't disturb the sleeping bear.

Gently place the bear back into her bag and send the children on to a quiet activity, like napping or silent reading.

Chapter Five
Storytelling with Puppets

One puppet, a carefully chosen story, and a skillful storyteller can create as much drama, excitement, and fun as a dozen puppets housed in a complex theatre. I know it sounds hard to believe, but it's *absolutely true*. This introduction provides tips on how to choose, learn, and tell stories with puppets. Scripts for using puppets to tell 10 complete stories follow this introduction.

WHAT PUPPETS TO USE

Hand puppets, finger puppets, pop-up puppets, or rod puppets work best for these scripts. Chapter 1 discusses these types of puppets in more detail. (See pages 5-6.)

WHAT STORIES WORK WELL

The challenge is finding a story with a character or characters that can be enhanced with puppet action performed by one person without a stage. Three types of stories lend themselves to this format. Perhaps the simplest tale is a story with only one character, like "The Teeny Tiny Woman." In this story, I use a finger puppet on a stick to pantomime the action as I tell the story.

Another effective story type is a story with two main characters. Because most puppeteers have two hands, both main characters can be puppets, with the storyteller doing voices and manipulation for them and narrating the rest. "The Gunny Wolf" is this type of story.

The most broad category of tale is the story with any number of characters, but with one character that can be brought to life by a puppet while the storyteller tells the rest of the story. I look for a character that has a significant part to play in the story as well as actions to do that can be accomplished either by a hand puppet or a finger puppet. Almost any collection of junk can be transformed into a troll to act in "The Three Billy Goats Gruff," with the storyteller playing all three goats and the narrator. In "The Little Red Hen and the Grain of Wheat," a hen puppet can act out all the hen's actions with the storyteller playing the cat, dog, mouse, and narrator. The possibilities are limited only by your time and imagination.

WHAT STORY TO USE FIRST

I have included scripts for many stories that will probably already be familiar to you. It will be much easier for you to add a puppet to a familiar story than to learn two new skills at once—how to tell an unfamiliar story and how to use a puppet in that telling.

Remember, even though a story is very familiar to you, it may be brand new to the children with whom you share it. Recently I was telling "Jack in the Beanstalk" to a group of about 25 children at a day care facility. Their ages ranged from kindergarten to third grade. Everyone was enjoying the story intently when I came to the part where Jack was escaping from the giant's wrath by climbing down the beanstalk with the hen that lays golden eggs safely tucked under his arm. As I finished reading that scene, a boy said excitedly, "Wouldn't that just be *so rad*!" In his imagination he was there, with Jack, on that beanstalk, feeling the excitement of escaping from the giant with the hen clutched under his arm.

The old story was brand new to that child. For him, the moment on the beanstalk was filled with the wonder that has caused this familiar story to live on through so many generations of tellers and listeners. So don't discount the old favorites. Bring them to life anew for new generations of eager imaginations.

Start with one of the story scripts in this section containing a story you already know so well that you can almost tell it without reading the script once. Follow the instructions for adding puppet action. Practice in front of a mirror, noticing all that the puppet can do to help bring its character, and the story, to life. As you work with the mirror, consider where the puppet will be during times that it is not in the story. Perhaps you could simply hold it behind your back. Perhaps it needs a bag or box or pocket in which to hide.

HOW TO CHOOSE A NEW STORY

After you've successfully added puppets to a story you already know, you may be ready to choose a story that you do not know. Use one of the scripts from this section that you aren't familiar with, or discover a new story to tell.

If you wish to discover a story on your own, search folktale collections, as folktales come from the oral tradition and beg to be told. When you've found a story that you *love,* a story that has one or two characters you can see being brought to life with puppets, you are ready to begin learning the story.

HOW TO LEARN A NEW STORY

Learn the story by heart, rather than memorizing the words. If you memorize the words, you may be in trouble if you forget where you are during the telling. When you learn the story by heart, you know the sequence of events and tell the story mostly in your own words. Then if you lose your place in the telling, you can pause for a moment, think about the event you were just describing, and you'll know what comes next.

If you are new to storytelling, plan to give yourself a minimum of one week to learn and become comfortable telling a story that is totally new to you. To learn the story, read it several times on different days. You may wish to tape-record the story so that you can listen to it in your car or at home. Each time you read or hear the story concentrate on one of the following elements of the story: characters, setting, sequence of events, and things you do wish to memorize.

As you imagine the characters and the setting, you will be learning more about them than you will actually tell your audiences. The more you know, the more alive your tale will be. Think of the setting using all five senses. How does the setting look, feel, smell, taste, and sound? If you are learning "The Gunny Wolf," for instance, picture the little girl's house. What color is it? How large is it? Is it neat and tidy with a white picket fence around the yard? Or is it more overgrown because mother is so busy being a single parent that she has no time for yard work? I imagine that there are no flowers in the yard, for if the little girl had flowers at home, she might not have been tempted into the forest by the flowers.

Now do the same thing for the forest. How does it smell? Are the trees so dense that it is dark and damp there? What kinds of trees and undergrowth are found there? Is the ground underfoot rough to walk on or soft with pine needles? Is the forest ominously silent or filled with bird songs? There are no right or wrong answers as you imagine the setting. Just use all of your senses to explore. Become familiar with what the setting is like so that you can bring the story alive as you tell it.

Ask the same kinds of questions about each character as you hear or read the story another time. If you already have puppets selected to use in telling the story, picture them in the action of the story. If you have not yet selected puppets, this preparation can help you either choose puppets to buy or design puppets to make for this tale. Is the little girl neatly dressed or disheveled and mischievous looking? What color is her hair? Is it curly or straight? How old is she? How does the Gunny Wolf look? How big is he in comparison to the girl? Does he smell bad? Is his fur rough or smooth, long or short? We know that he moves in a clumsy, crashing fashion to the sound of "hunker che . . . hunker che."

On your third time through the story, you may wish to make notes on the sequence of events and the few items you want to memorize. Carry these notes with you to refer to as you practice your story throughout the week. Items you need to memorize include:

1. repeated refrains, such as "Run, run, as fast as you can. You can't catch *me!* I'm the Gingerbread Man!"

2. repeated lists, such as the order of colors of caps the peddler repeatedly puts on his head in *Caps for Sale* by Slobodkin.

3. repeated phrases, such as "'Very well then, I'll do it myself,' said the Little Red Hen. And she did."

4. selected words that create the flavor of the language of the original tale or the country of origin. The Gunny Wolf repeatedly says, "Little Girl, why for you move?" And the little girl always answers, "Oh, I no move."

5. important rhymes and spells, even if they are only stated once in the story.

Practice telling the story out loud several times, going back to your original for reassurance that you are including everything you planned to include.

HOW TO ADD PUPPET ACTION

After you know the story well enough to tell it comfortably, you are ready to add the puppet character to your telling. Concentrate on how the puppet can *show through action*, as well as words, what is happening in the story. Practice with the puppet in front of a mirror first, and then try it out on folks who are willing to give you feedback.

Enjoy this technique of bringing a story to life with puppets. Remember, if you love the story and enjoy sharing it, the children will love it, too.

THE TEENY TINY WOMAN
English

Characters/Themes: Scary Creatures, Food, Surprises

Ages: 3 to 8

Puppet Needed: You will need a finger puppet or a hand puppet of a teeny tiny woman.

Picture Book Version: Seuling, Barbara. *The Teeny Tiny Woman.* Illustrated by Paul Galdone. New York: Viking, 1976.

The teeny tiny woman goes for a walk in the teeny tiny forest.

Instructions: This story is a good choice to tell with a puppet because there is only one character, the teeny tiny woman herself. It is a traditional "jump" tale, with the storyteller making the audience jump at the end by loudly saying the final words of the teeny tiny woman while swiftly thrusting the puppet toward the audience.

The tale can be made more or less scary through the way it is told. Suspense can be added for primary grade children through strategic pauses and an increasingly eerie tone as the story progresses. Conversely, it is also an appropriate story for preschoolers if told in a very matter-of-fact way with emphasis on the silliness of the repetition of the words "teeny tiny" and a less startling "jump" at the end.

For small groups of up to 30 children, try using a teeny tiny woman finger puppet on a stick. You can get more different types of movement from her when she's on a stick than if she is actually on your finger. It's fun to use a finger puppet because the character really *is* a teeny tiny woman. For groups of more than 30, however, it is better to use a hand puppet so all can see. Even a hand puppet is a teeny tiny woman compared to a real woman.

Tell the story while using the puppet to pantomime the action; use dialogue only when the teeny tiny woman finds the bone and says what she plans to do with it and during the conversation between the teeny tiny woman and the voice from the teeny tiny cupboard.

Introduction

What to Say

Boys and girls, someone special is going to help me tell this story. Let me see if she is ready to begin.

What to Do

Get the teeny tiny woman puppet out of your hiding place (a bag, box, pocket, or drawer) and hold her behind your back, hiding her from audience.

The Story

Once there was a teeny tiny woman who lived in a teeny tiny house right near the edge of a teeny tiny forest.

The teeny tiny woman walks out from behind your back and takes a bow as you say the first line.

One day the teeny tiny woman decided to go for a teeny tiny walk. She went out of her teeny tiny house, through her teeny tiny gate, carefully closing it behind her, and into the teeny tiny forest.

She pantomimes these actions as you say them. Create a ground level in your own mind and keep that consistent throughout the action of the story as the teeny tiny woman pantomimes walking into and out of the forest.

She had only walked a teeny tiny ways into the teeny tiny forest when she looked down near her teeny tiny feet and saw a teeny tiny bone.

She pantomimes walking back and forth on a zigzag course until she sees the bone. Bring your free hand up, palm out flat; that is where she looks down at the imaginary teeny tiny bone.

"Oh, look," she said. "This teeny tiny bone will make a delicious teeny tiny soup for my teeny tiny supper."

As she speaks, she moves a little bit back and forth to help the audience "see" that she is talking. Her voice is high-pitched (but not squeaky) to show she is small.

And she bent down a teeny tiny ways, picked up the teeny tiny bone, and started back through the teeny tiny forest to her teeny tiny house.

She actually bends down and pretends to pick up the bone from your hand before turning to make her return journey.

She walked through her teeny tiny gate, carefully, closing it behind her, up her teeny tiny walk, and into her teeny tiny house. She put the teeny tiny bone into her teeny tiny cupboard

When you pantomime putting away the teeny tiny bone, pretend the teeny tiny cupboard is on the opposite side of your body from where the teeny tiny woman will go to sleep on your shoulder. That way when she peeks out from her bed to look toward the teeny tiny voice coming from the teeny tiny cupboard, we know the voice is not *too* close to her.

The teeny tiny woman notices a teeny tiny bone on the forest floor.

The teeny tiny woman pantomimes picking up the teeny tiny bone from your free hand.

Now the teeny tiny woman was a teeny tiny bit tired so she went up her teeny tiny stairs, climbed into her teeny tiny bed, and went to sleep.

When the teeny tiny woman goes to sleep, use your body for her bed, cuddling her to sleep on your shoulder with your free hand acting as the covers. Turn her back to the audience so her eyes are not visible. The children love it if you make her snore softly once or twice each time she goes to sleep.

She had been asleep but a teeny tiny time when she heard a teeny tiny voice say, "Give me my bone."

Since the voice is coming from the cupboard, the teeny tiny woman does not move as the voice speaks. This helps the audience "see" that the voice is not coming from her. The voice speaks in a soft, eerie tone.

Well, the teeny tiny woman was a teeny tiny bit frightened, but she pulled her teeny tiny head a teeny tiny bit farther under the teeny tiny covers and went back to sleep. [Snores]

As you say these lines, the teeny tiny woman peeks out from under your hand, shivers, and pulls her head a little farther back out of sight under your hand, again turning away from the audience.

She had been asleep but a teeny tiny bit longer when she heard a teeny tiny voice a teeny tiny bit louder say, "Give me my bone."

Say "Give me my bone" a little louder and more insistently than you said it the first time.

Well, the teeny tiny woman was a teeny tiny bit more frightened, but she pulled her teeny tiny head a teeny tiny bit farther down under the teeny tiny covers and went back to sleep. [Snores]

The teeny tiny woman once more peeks out from under your hand, shivers, and pulls her head even farther back out of sight.

She had been asleep but a teeny tiny bit longer when she heard a teeny tiny voice a teeny tiny bit louder say, "GIVE ME MY BONE!"

Say "Give me my bone!" *very loudly* this time.

Well, the teeny tiny woman was a teeny tiny bit more frightened, but this time she pulled her teeny tiny head our from under her teeny tiny covers and said in her loudest teeny tiny voice, "TAKE IT!"

The teeny tiny woman rises up from under your hand, still shivering, and then jumps toward the audience as she shouts "TAKE IT!"

And that's the story of the teeny tiny woman.

The teeny tiny woman takes a bow and walks behind your back once more.

WIDE-MOUTHED FROG
Traditional

Characters/Themes: Ecology, Humor, Jungle Beasts, Food

Ages: 4 to 8

Source: I learned this story from Nancy Schimmel, storyteller and songwriter. There is also at least one picture book version of the story, listed below:

Schneider, Rex. *The Wide-Mouthed Frog.* Owings Mills, MD: Stemmer House Publishers, 1980.

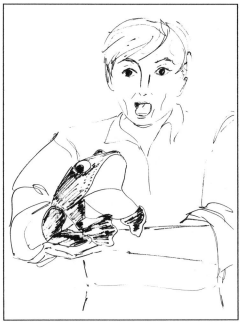

For most of the story the frog speaks with a very wide-open mouth to emphasize the fact that she is a wide-mouth frog.

Voices: The frog's voice must be distinctive from your storyteller voice. Experiment with making the frog's vowel sounds drawn out, as if it takes them an extra long time to emerge from her wide mouth. Imagine that she is from the South, with a slow, Southern rate of speech. Check Chapter 8 under "Puppet Voices" for more hints on finding an appropriate voice. Note that she will say her final lines quickly with her tiny mouth.

Puppet Needed: For this you will need a frog puppet with a flexible mouth that can be opened wide and also be opened a very little bit for the last lines at the end of the story. You may quickly make one out of paper using the instructions for "Wide-Mouthed Frog" in the children's activities, Section 2 of this book. (See page 111.) When you have read the story, you will understand why the frog's mouth movements are so important.

Instructions: Practice with your frog puppet in the mirror to see how she looks sitting on the arm of your chair, or on your arm, as you converse with her. See how she should move as she hops on to meet the other animals in the story. You may want her to hop along your forearm, held parallel to the ground and a little away from your body. When she finishes her third hop each time, she should be back in a place that's comfortable for you to hold her and speak with her.

Next, play with the movement of her mouth, exaggerating it to create as wide-mouthed an appearance as you can. Watch in the mirror as you practice coordinating her wide-mouthed movements with her words. Then make her mouth as tiny as you can to practice saying her final lines in the story.

The Story

What to Say

Storyteller: I've got a wide-mouthed frog friend here I'd like you to meet. She has something very important to tell you.

Ms. Frog, tell the boys and girls your exciting news.

Frog: Boys and girls, I have some brand new babies! They are the most wonderful babies in the whole world.

In fact, my babies are so wonderful, they are too good to eat the flies and mosquitoes frog babies usually eat. They need something better.

Storyteller: Well, what will you feed them?

Frog: I am going on a journey to ask other mothers what they feed their babies. I am sure I will get some ideas about what to feed mine.

What to Do

Reach inside your bag to put on the frog puppet. Bring her out with an enthusiastic hop and settle her onto your forearm or the arm of your chair.

You and frog look at each other as you speak, and she nods "yes."

She looks at the audience. Be sure to use her wide-mouthed frog voice and wide-mouthed movements as she speaks.

She looks back at you and speaks in a very boastful manner.

Sound puzzled as you look at her and ask your question.

Frog sounds very determined and nods "yes" emphatically.

Storyteller: And so the wide-mouthed frog began her journey through the swamp . . . hop . . . hop . . . hop.

Frog hops once each time you say the word "hop," landing again in a comfortable place to speak to you and out toward the audience.

Soon she came to a turtle.

Have the frog look toward an imaginary turtle.

Frog: Ms. Turtle, Ms. Turtle, what do you feed your babies?

As she speaks, emphasize her wide mouth.

Storyteller: The turtle answered, "I feed my babies on these tender mushrooms."

Frog looks down a bit toward the imaginary mushrooms and scrunches up her mouth in disgust.

Frog: Well, those mushrooms smell a little earthy for me. Thank you. I'll keep looking.

Frog makes sniffing noises and nose movements toward the imaginary mushrooms before speaking.

Storyteller: And so the wide-mouthed frog continued her journey through the swamp . . . hop . . . hop . . . hop.

Frog hops once each time you say the word "hop."

Soon she came to a deer.

She hops back a bit, for the imaginary deer is very large.

Frog: Ms. Deer, Ms. Deer, what do you feed your babies?

She sounds very hopeful.

Storyteller: The deer replied, "I feed my babies on the tender new shoots at the tops of the trees."

Frog's mouth hangs open slightly as she hears this.

Frog: I could never climb trees to reach that food for my babies. Thank you. I'll keep looking.

She shakes her head "no."

Storyteller: And so the wide-mouthed frog continued her journey through the swamp . . . hop . . . hop . . . hop.

Frog makes the three hops as you say them.

Next she came to an owl, high up in a tree.

Frog slowly stretches her neck to look high above her toward the imaginary owl.

Frog: Ms. Owl, Ms. Owl, what do you feed your babies?

Frog calls upward toward the owl.

Storyteller: The owl hooted and replied, "I feed my babies on fine, fresh mice."

Frog again scrunches up her face in disgust.

Frog: I could never catch a mouse for my babies. Thank you. I'll keep looking.

Frog shakes her head "no."

Storyteller: And so the wide-mouthed frog continued her journey through the swamp . . . hop . . . hop . . . hop.

Frog makes the three hops as you say them.

She hopped to the edge of the wide river. There swimming toward her, was a . . . large crocodile. Loudly, she called out to the crocodile.

You and frog look off into the distance toward the imaginary crocodile.

Frog: Ms. Crocodile, Ms. Crocodile, what do you feed your babies?

Make this line the loudest with the most exaggerated wide mouth you can create.

Storyteller: Still swimming toward her, the crocodile called out, "I feed my babies on wide . . . mouthed . . . frogs!

Frog takes a hop back in astonishment, looks around quickly, and recovers her composure.

The frog made her mouth as small as she could when she replied to the crocodile, "Oh. Well. Thank you very much."

Frog: Oh. Well. Thank you very much.

Say this very quickly, using tiny mouth movements.

Storyteller: And the narrow-mouthed frog hopped away as quickly as ever she could. Hop! Hop! Hop!

On the third hop, make frog hop out of sight behind your back.

In disgust, the crocodile turned around and swam away.

You watch her go for a second before speaking.

Boys and girls, that crocodile swam off, and I see no other crocodiles in the river now. I think it's safe to ask the frog to come back out now.

Look all around and then back toward the audience, to show you've thoroughly looked for the crocodile.

Ms. Frog, Ms. Frog, will you come out? The crocodile has gone.

Turn your head in the direction the frog went when she disappeared. Frog hops back out, landing on your forearm.

Frog: Thank goodness that terrible beast is gone.

She speaks with her old wide-mouthed movements, but she sounds very relieved and a bit humbled.

Storyteller: Ms. Frog, Ms. Frog, what will you feed your babies?

Look at the frog and ask this question in a manner similar to the way the frog had asked the other mothers. Put a bit of a chuckle in your voice.

Frog: Oh, I'll feed my babies on delicious flies and mosquitoes . . . the perfect food for wide-mouthed frogs!

She has a chuckle in her voice too, as she answers your question.

Storyteller: And the wide-mouthed frog went home to feed her babies . . . hop . . . hop . . . hop.

On the third hop, have the frog hop back into the bag where she will stay while you and the children go on to the next activity.

THE LITTLE RED HEN AND THE GRAIN OF WHEAT
English

Characters/Themes: Chickens, Food, Friends.

Ages: 2 to 5

Puppet Needed: A little red hen hand puppet or finger puppet is the only puppet used in this script. You can make a head for a hen from a styrofoam ball by adding eyes, a beak, and a comb to the ball and putting in a hole for your thumb. Put a glove on your hand and the hen head on your thumb as pictured in the illustration, and you will have created a very effective Little Red Hen puppet. See Chapter 10 for places to buy commercial hen puppets if you do not wish to make your own.

Voices: The little red hen must speak for herself. Her voice should be noticeably different from the storyteller's voice. Most of the time she will sound very matter-of-fact, occasionally she may sound exasperated, and her last lines will be spoken with a hint of glee.

It is not necessary, but it adds to the fun to also have slightly different voices for the cat, the dog, and the mouse. The cat's could have a hint of a "meow" undertone. The dog's would be lower and rough. The mouse's would be the highest voice of all with just a hint of a squeak. As you develop their voices, you might begin by saying "meow" before speaking for the cat, "woof" before speaking for the dog, and "squeak" before speaking for the mouse. This may help you in creating their different voices. If you need more help, read about voice development and voice anchors in Chapter 8.

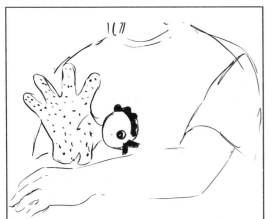

The little red hen is made from a glove and a styrofoam ball.

The cat, the dog, and the mouse all sound very tired and unenthusiastic each time they say "Not I." They sound excited only at the very end when they are happy about the idea of eating cake and all say "I will!"

Instructions: Because it has so much repetition, this story is easy to learn. Once you know the story, adding puppet action is very easy. The basic idea is that you, the storyteller, pretend to play all the parts in the story except the part of the little red hen. Have the little red hen puppet turn slightly toward you and speak to you as if you are the other characters in the story.

Throughout the play, the little red hen pantomimes all her actions as the narrator describes them, so it is easy to know what the puppet should be doing. As she is walking about, remember to keep her the same height at all times to create the illusion that she is walking on the ground. You may wish to use your free arm to represent the ground, holding it in front of you, bent at the elbow, and parallel to the ground so the little red hen can appear to be walking on it. Practice in front of a mirror and choose what looks best and is most comfortable for you.

After you learn the sequence of events in the story, you should spend a little time on voices. Practice the story with the puppet action and voices once or twice in front of a mirror. Then you will be ready to perform for the children.

Introduction

What to Say	**What to Do**
Storyteller: Children, I am going to use a puppet to help me tell this story. Wait a second while I see if she is ready to help.	Turn your back on the children and put the little red hen on your hand. Quickly turn back to face the children, hiding the puppet behind your back.

The Story

Storyteller: Once upon a time a little red hen lived with a very sleepy dog, a tired cat, and a slow moving mouse.	Have the little red hen walk out from behind your back.
One day when the little red hen was out walking, she found a grain of wheat.	Hold your free hand out flat, palm up, so she can look down and find the imaginary wheat in your hand.
Little Red Hen: Oh look, a grain of wheat! I'll take it home and see what to do with it.	She speaks cheerfully as she bends down and picks up the imaginary wheat in her beak.
Storyteller: So the little red hen took the grain of wheat home. Then she asked a question of her companions, a dog, a cat and a mouse.	She turns and walks back in the direction from which she came.
Little Red Hen: Who will help me plant this wheat?	Have the hen turn slightly to look at you as she asks the question, because you will answer for the dog, cat, and mouse.
Dog: Woof, not I.	Remember to sound very tired as you say their lines to the hen. You may even want to shake your head "no" at times.
Cat: Meow, not I.	
Mouse: Squeak, not I.	
Little Red Hen: Very well then, I'll do it myself.	She nods "yes."
Storyteller: And she did. Ever so carefully, the little red hen chose a good spot and dug a hole in the ground. She gently placed the wheat in the hole, covering it up with soft earth.	Hold out your free hand, palm up, to represent the ground where the hen is working. In pantomime, have her look around, choose a spot, pretend to dig with her beak, pick up the grain, place it in the hole, and cover the spot while you as storyteller describe these actions.
She looked at her work with satisfaction and returned home to her companions. The very next morning she asked the dog, the cat, and the mouse a new question.	She looks down at her work for a second, before turning to walk back to her house.
Little Red Hen: Who will help me care for this wheat?	Again, the hen looks at you as she speaks.
Dog: Woof, not I.	The dog yawns as he speaks. All three sound very tired.
Cat: Meow, not I.	

Mouse: Squeak, not I.

Little Red Hen: Very well then, I'll do it myself.

She nods "yes."

Storyteller: And she did. Every day the little red hen watered the wheat and pulled weeds from around it. Every day the wheat grew a little taller, until one day the little red hen decided the wheat was ready for harvest. She went home to her companions.

Pantomime the actions you describe, again using your free palm to represent the area where the wheat is growing.

Little Red Hen: Who will help me harvest this wheat?

The hen looks at you as she asks for help.

Dog: Woof, not I.

This time, the dog and cat both yawn as they answer. All three sound verrrrry tired.

Cat: Meow, not I.

Mouse: Squeak, not I.

Little Red Hen: Very well then, I'll do it myself.

She nods "yes."

Storyteller: And she did. The little red hen carefully harvested the grain, not losing a single kernel. When she was finished, she carried the grain back to her house and asked for help again.

Use your free palm again to show where the wheat is growing. The hen uses her beak to pull up the imaginary wheat and then walks back to her house.

Little Red Hen: Who will help me take this wheat to the mill to be ground into flour?

She looks at you.

Dog: Woof, not I.

All three yawn before speaking and sound very unenthusiastic.

Cat: Meow, not I.

Mouse: Squeak, not I.

Little Red Hen: Very well then, I'll do it myself.

She nods "yes."

Storyteller: And she did. The little red hen carried the grain to the mill where it was ground into white flour. When she carried the flour home, she found the dog, the cat, and the mouse fast asleep.

Make the little red hen walk a zigzag course away from you as she pretends to take the grain to the mill. On her way home, she zigzags back toward you.

Loudly, she asked for help.

Snoring is heard as she arrives home.

Little Red Hen: Who will help me use this flour to make a cake?

She looks at you and speaks with exaggerated loudness.

Dog: Woof, not I.

Yawning, they sound almost annoyed as they answer.

Cat: Meow, not I.

Mouse: Squeak, not I.

Little Red Hen: Very well then, I'll do it myself.

She nods "yes."

Storyteller: And she did. The little red hen mixed the flour with lots of good ingredients and soon the cake was baking. Wonderful smells filled the house. At last the dog and the cat and the mouse got up from their resting places. They gathered around the good smells coming from the stove. Very soon the cake was done.

Sound very eager as you talk about the animals getting up to gather around the imaginary stove.

The little red hen took the cake from the oven and placed it on the table. Then she asked another question.

The hen pantomimes taking the cake from the oven with her beak and setting it on an imaginary table.

Little Red Hen: Who will help me eat this cake?

Dog: Woof! I will!

Speak with great enthusiasm.

Cat: Meow! I will!

Mouse: Squeak! I will!

Little Red Hen: Oh no you won't. All by myself I planted this wheat. All by myself I tended the wheat, harvested it, and took it to the mill to be ground into flour. All by myself I made the flour into this fine cake, and all by myself I will eat it!

Say the first line slowly and deliberately. Speak firmly but with a hint of glee.

Storyteller: And she did, down to the very last crumb. She called her baby chicks, and the little red hen and her chicks ate and ate and ate until the cake was all gone.

The little red hen pantomimes calling her chicks and eating cake from the palm of your hand.

And that is the story of " ʳ ᶦᵗᵗle Red Hen and the Grain of Wheat."

Then the little red hen takes a bow and walks behind your back out of sight.

THE TORTOISE AND THE HARE
Fable

Characters/Theme: Turtles, Perseverance, Jungle Beasts

Ages: 6 to 8

Puppets Needed: You will need hand puppets or finger puppets for the hare and the tortoise. The instructions in the script for this story assume that you are using two puppets.

You could also develop this story using just one of the two characters, either the tortoise or the hare. Read the scripts for "The Little Red Hen and the Grain of Wheat" and "Wide-Mouth Frog" to get an idea of how a story with more than one character may be told by a storyteller using a single puppet.

Voices and Movement: Bringing out the essence of the two characters is essential to the effectiveness of the story. The hare must always move quickly, although at times he may move erratically. To help emphasize his quickness, have him speak quickly as well. Try adding a nasal quality to the hare's swift speech patterns to give him an even more distinct way of talking. Noises can also add a lot to this character. When he's boasting about his speed, he can punctuate his sentences with noises similar to those children make when they are playing racing cars—a brrrumm, brruuum sound.

In contrast, the tortoise always moves ver-r-r-y slowly and deliberately. Her speech should also be used to emphasize these characteristics. Try making her speech so slow that there is a slight hesitation between each word.

As you practice the puppet movements, remember to keep the puppets the same distance from the floor as you manipulate them. This creates the illusion that they are walking, hopping, and running on the ground. If you feel that everyone in your group can see, you may use a table for the ground. Sit in a chair behind the table, and during the race, have the hare hop along the edge of the table nearest you and the tortoise crawl along the tabletop.

Introduction

What to Say

Storyteller: Now I'm going to have some puppets help me tell the next story. Stay right there while I see if they are ready to help.

This is a story about two very different characters. Here comes the first one.

What to Do

Turn your back briefly while you put the puppets on. Then turn quickly to face the children while holding both puppets behind your back.

Hare hops out swiftly from behind your back.

The Story

Hare: I am the fastest runner in this neck of the woods, that's for sure! And I do believe I'm getting faster every day. Brrumm, brrumm, brruuuum!! No one has ever beaten me in a race. No one ever has, and no one ever will!

The hare speaks in a very animated and boastful way with lots of gestures and occasional hops for emphasis.

Tortoise: I will race you.

The tortoise slowly walks out from behind your back, stops for a moment, and carefully looks up and down at the upright and agitated rabbit. She speaks in a lower, very slow voice.

As the animals talk, have them half turn toward each other so they appear to be speaking to each other while their faces are still visible to the audience.

Hare: Ha! You, race me? I would leave you in the dust! I would run circles around you! I would *win*! Why would you want to race me?

He is still moving quickly and speaking boastfully.

Tortoise: Never mind why. When shall we race?

She looks at the hare as she slowly speaks.

Hare: Well, if you are sure that you want to be humiliated by losing a race very badly, meet me here tomorrow at one o'clock.

He bounces around as he speaks.

Tortoise: I'll be here.

The tortoise slowly walks behind your back in one direction, while the hare swiftly hops away behind your back in the other direction.

Storyteller: A racecourse had been marked, and all was ready by one o'clock the next day. All the animals of the forest gathered to watch the race.

Look around you as you talk about the animals, as if you are looking at them all gathered to watch the race.

Tortoise: I am ready now.

The tortoise slowly walks out from behind your back and into her place.

68

Storyteller: It is one o'clock, Tortoise, and you are here. But where is the hare?

You and the tortoise look around the room.

If he is not here in five minutes, he must forfeit the race.

Look at the tortoise, who nods "yes" slowly.

All the animals waited. Four and a half minutes later the hare arrived, a bit out of breath.

Tortoise slowly taps her foot to show that they are waiting a long time.

Hare: Sorry I'm late. Lost track of the time.

Hare hops swiftly out and looks at you as if you are in charge of the race.

Hare: Are you ready for defeat, Tortoise?

Hare looks at the tortoise

Tortoise: I am ready to begin the race.

She speaks as slowly as ever.

Storyteller: The two animals lined up at the starting line.

Place the tortoise and the hare side by side at about your waist height, facing the audience.

All together, the crowd of animals called out, "Ready, Set, Go!" The hare darted away from the finish line, leaving the tortoise far behind!

At the word "Go!" the hare swiftly hops forward while zigzagging to the right and left.

Finally, the hare was so far ahead of the tortoise that he stopped along the way to take a rest. He closed his eyes for just a minute, and he went right to sleep. He slept peacefully for a long time.

Have the hare settle down in a comfortable place and go to sleep. Place him with his paws over his eyes or his head turned away from the audience so his open eyes do not show. Children usually love it if you make him snore.

Verrrry slowly, the tortoise was walking down the race course through the dust the hare had raised. Steadily, she walked right past the sleeping hare, keeping her eyes on the finish line.

Make the tortoise walk slowly, following the zigzag path the hare took. She does not look at the hare when she passes him.

When the hare woke up, he felt startled.

The hare sits up swiftly.

Hare: Wasn't I in a race this afternoon?

The hare looks toward the tortoise, who is still slowly walking, almost at the end of your arm's length.

Hare: I remember! I was racing the tortoise, and there she goes . . . across the finish line! Oh, no!

The hare puts his face in his paws, his head down, and slowly hops out of sight behind your back.

Storyteller: All the animals cheered for the tortoise as she crossed the finish line and took a bow.

The tortoise looks up from her persistent plodding and takes a bow.

Tortoise: As you can see, sometimes slow and steady wins the race.

The tortoise speaks to the children and then slowly walks out of sight behind your back.

THE GUNNY WOLF
African-American

Characters/Themes: Scary Creatures, Wolves

Ages: 3 to 8

Puppets Needed: Little girl and Gunny Wolf hand puppets are needed for this story. You can play the part of the mother without using a puppet by speaking the mother's lines directly to the little girl puppet.

Because no one knows what a Gunny Wolf looks like, you may use a commercial wolf puppet or another unusual creature to play the part. Just be sure the Gunny Wolf does not look too scary if you are performing for preschoolers. Choosing the Gunny Wolf's character carefully can also help control how scary he is. Through action and voice he can be very menacing or just a mildly threatening bumbler.

Voices: The little girl's voice is higher, young, yet decisive. Gunny Wolf's voice is lower. If you are performing for preschoolers, have him sound kind of bumbling and hollow rather than menacing. Mother's voice should sound mature, somewhere between the little girl and the Gunny Wolf in pitch.

Instructions: Use a mirror to practice in pantomime the actions your puppets will be making. Show the little girl playing in her house, in her yard, and right near the edge of the forest. Show her singing as she walks into the forest. Show the Gunny Wolf jumping up to frighten her; as he appears, she begins to tremble. Also with the Gunny Wolf, practice very exaggerated ways for him to go to sleep on your shoulder—yawning, stretching, searching for the most comfortable place, and finally snoring. Be sure his eyes are out of the audience's sight when he's sleeping.

The repeated chase is an important opportunity for action. In the mirror, look at the different ways the puppets can run. Keep them at a consistent height and use a zigzag course to add more length to the chase. Little girl runs with quick, small steps, "pit pat, pit pat." Gunny Wolf chases her with lumbering jumps, "hunker che, hunker che."

Introduction

What to Say	**What to Do**
Storyteller: I'm going to tell you a very special story. Wait just a minute while I see if the puppets are ready to help me.	**Turn your back to the children and put on the puppets. Then quickly turn back to face the children, hiding the puppets behind your back.**

The Story

Once there was a little girl who lived with her mother in a house right near the edge of the forest.	**Have the little girl walk out from behind your back and nod to the audience.**
One day her mother had to go into town to do some shopping. Before she left, she said, "Little girl, you may play anywhere you like in our house and in our yard. But remember, don't go into that forest. If you do, the Gunny Wolf might get you!"	**Have the little girl look at you as you deliver the mother's lines. Give special attention to the last line, pausing after "do" and emphasizing "might."**
Little Girl: Oh no, Mother, I won't.	**The little girl looks at you and shakes her head "no."**
Storyteller: So the little girl's mother left to go to town.	**The little girl looks off into the distance and waves good-bye as if waving to her mother.**

For a while the little girl was happy playing in the house. Then she went out to play in the sunshine in the yard. After a time, she found herself near the edge of the yard and right next to the deep, dark forest.

Pantomime playing motions with the little girl—first to your right, then near the center of your body, then a little to the left—to show the different areas where the little girl plays as she nears the forest.

Have her stop and look toward an imaginary forest.

From where she was standing, she could see a little ways into the forest. There, in a small clearing, were some beautiful white flowers.

Little Girl: "Oh, those flowers look so pretty.

She claps her hands while looking toward the imaginary flowers. She also moves her head slightly to show she is talking.

I think I'll go just a little ways into the forest, pick just one flower, and come right back out. I'll keep my eyes open, and I'm sure it will be all right."

She nods her head "yes."

Storyteller: And so she went, and as she went, she sang, "Kum ka ki wah, kum ka ki wah."

As she pantomimes walking into the forest, she also moves her head from side to side as she sings, in time with the music. She walks a zigzag path, first to your right and then back to your left.

She picked the white flower. Then from where she was standing just a little ways into the forest, she could see a bit farther into the forest, and there she saw a small clearing filled with beautiful red flowers.

Pantomime bending down and picking a flower, then standing and looking a little farther into the forest.

Little Girl: "Oh, those red flowers are even more beautiful than these white ones. And a red one and a white one would look so nice on our table together.

Have her jump up and down, but don't clap her hands or she'll drop the imaginary white flower she is already holding!

I think I'll just go a little farther into the forest and pick a red flower. I'll keep my eyes open, and I'm sure it will be all right."

She nods her head "yes."

Storyteller: And so she went, and as she went, she sang, "Kum ka ki wah, kum ka ki wah."

Have her move her head in time with her music as she sings and walks farther into the forest.

She picked the red flower.

Pantomime bending over to pick the red flower, then standing up to peer farther into the forest.

Now from where she was standing, she could see into the very middle of the forest, and there she saw some beautiful purple flowers.

Speak with wonder in your voice.

Little Girl: "Oh, those purple flowers are the most beautiful of all. Besides, a purple one would look just lovely with the red and white ones I already have picked. I'll put them in a vase on our table. Mother will be so pleased.

Put extra pleasure in the little girl's voice as she says "purple flowers." Have her take a few steps back, to show her astonishment at their color.

I'm just going a little farther into the forest to pick one purple flower. I'll keep my eyes open, and I'm sure it will be all right."

She nods "yes" with determination.

Storyteller: And so she went into the very middle of the forest, and as she went, she sang, "Kum ka ki wah, kum ka ki wah."

Say "And so she went into the very middle of the forest" slowly, with apprehension in your voice. Again, pantomime her walking a zigzag path farther into the forest, a little more slowly this time as the forest is getting even deeper and darker. She is still moving her head in time with her singing.

Just as she bent to pick a purple flower, up jumped the Gunny Wolf!

As the little girl bends down, quickly bring the Gunny Wolf out from behind your back as you say loudly and with surprise in your voice, "Up jumped the Gunny Wolf!" When she sees him, she jumps back a bit and trembles in fright.

During the dialogue below, the puppets face each other, slightly turned in the direction of the audience so their faces are still visible to the children as they speak to each other. Remember, the one who is talking should move slightly, and the one who is listening should be still, except for light movements in reaction to the speaker. For example, the little girl could tremble in fright as the Gunny Wolf speaks.

Concentrate on giving the Gunny Wolf a slightly lower and slower voice than the little girl's. (You can judge how scary the wolf's voice should be by the ages and reactions of the children in the audience as the story progresses.)

Note that during the dialogue between the little girl and the Gunny Wolf, you do not need to say "he said" and "she said." You will indicate which puppet is speaking by using the appropriate voice and moving only the puppet who is talking. The other puppet is standing still and listening.

Gunny Wolf: "Little girl, why for you move?"

Little Girl: "Oh, I no move."

Gunny Wolf: "Then you sing that goodest, sweetest song again, all right?"

Storyteller: Well, she was frightened, but she sang, "Kum ka ki wah, kum ka ki wah . . ."

Down went the Gunny Wolf's head, and he was fast asleep.

Pantomime this action, having the wolf fall asleep on your left shoulder, snuggling in and turning his head so his eyes are not visible to the audience.

Little girl began to run . . . pit pat, pit pat.

The little girl can run a zigzag course in front of you, to give more length and excitement to these chase scenes.

But he woke up and he ran after her . . . hunker che, hunker che, hunker che . . .

Have the little girl run with smaller steps, bobbing up and down rapidly as she moves forward. The wolf moves with larger, lumbering jumps.

and he *caught* her!

Make the action match your words, so that the wolf reaches out and grabs the little girl as you say the words "and he caught her!" When he does catch her, use one swift move to bring both puppets back close to your body so they will have room to run again.

Gunny Wolf: "Little girl, why for you move?"

Indicate who is talking by movement and voice.

Little Girl: "Oh, I no move."

Gunny Wolf: "Then you sing that goodest, sweetest song again, all right?"

Storyteller: Well, she was even more frightened, but she sang, "Kum ka ki wah, kum ka ki wah . . ."

This time, her voice and body tremble a little as she sings.

Down went the Gunny Wolf's head, and he was fast asleep again.

Take a little longer for him to fall asleep this time. Perhaps he yawns and stretches before lying down in his place on your shoulder and turning his head so his eyes are not visible. He can snore softly.

Little girl began to run again . . . pit pat, pit pat.

Looking at the wolf to make sure he's asleep before she leaves, the little girl runs another zigzag course.

But he woke up and he ran after her . . . hunker che, hunker che, hunker che . . .

and he *caught* her!

Again, show the little girl running with smaller steps, the wolf with larger, lumbering jumps. Make the action match your words, so that the wolf reaches out and grabs the little girl as you say "and he caught her!" Bring them both back in front of you with one swift movement.

Gunny Wolf: Little girl, why for you move?

Gunny Wolf sounds disgusted. Little girl still sounds and acts frightened.

Little Girl: "Oh, I no move."

Gunny Wolf: "Then you sing that goodest, sweetest song again, all right?"

Storyteller: Well, she was even more frightened, but she sang, "Kum ka ki wah, kum ka ki wah . . ."

Little girl trembles as she sings, watching the Gunny Wolf all the time.

Down went the Gunny Wolf's head,

The Gunny Wolf takes even longer to fall asleep this time, yawning and stretching several times before lying down. The Gunny Wolf might even look up at the girl after hiding his face, yawn again, and hide his face once more. Throughout this action, little girl keeps singing more and more sweetly.

and he was fast asleep again.

Finally he begins to snore again. Watching carefully, little girl sings even longer until she knows he is sleeping more deeply than ever before. Take your time with this scene; the audience loves it.

The little girl began to run once more. Pit pat, pit pat she ran through the forest, pit pat, pit pat past the red flowers, pit pat, pit pat past the white flowers, pit pat, pit pat across her yard . . .

Pantomime this running in a zigzag line as before, having the little girl occasionally look behind her toward the wolf and then keep on running. This time you are talking faster, with an even greater sense of urgency, and she is running even faster than before.

and pit pat, pit pat into her very own house where she slammed the door!

When she runs into her very own house, have her run out of sight behind your back.

She was goodest, sweetest safe.

Make your voice sound very satisfied and speak a little more slowly as you say this line.

As for that Gunny Wolf, when he woke up he did not see the little girl anywhere around. He wandered off, still trying to remember the goodest, sweetest song the little girl had been singing.

And that is the story of the little girl and the Gunny Wolf.

The Gunny Wolf wakes up startled and looks all around. As he wanders out of sight behind your back, singing his funny, mixed-up version of the little girl's song, have him shake his head in confusion.

You may wish to bring little girl and Gunny Wolf out from behind your back so they can take a bow as you say this line.

Turn away from the audience again to take the puppets off your hands and put them away out of sight, and begin the next activity.

BAD HABITS
West African

Characters/Themes: Friends, Humor, Jungle Beasts

Ages: 4 to 8

Puppets Needed: You will need rabbit and monkey hand puppets. This tale can also be told using only one of the characters, with you, the storyteller, playing the part of the other character. Using only one puppet may be easier for a beginning teller than using two puppets. See "Wide-Mouthed Frog" and "The Little Red Hen and the Grain of Wheat" scripts for examples of how to use a single puppet in a story with several characters.

Voices: If you do use two puppets, work toward having a different voice for each character as well as a different voice for you, the storyteller. You may wish to speak in your natural voice as the storyteller and alter your voice for the puppets. Try a quick, mischievous voice for the monkey and a slightly softer, slower voice for the rabbit.

Instructions: Practice with your puppets in front of a mirror. You will want to keep them at a consistent height. Sitting in a chair with arms may help you do this if you rest one of the animals on each arm of the chair. You may wish to try this if you think the audience can all see if you are sitting down.

If you need to stand to tell the story, try resting your elbows against your sides. This will help keep your arms from getting tired as well as help keep the puppets at a consistent height.

You will also want to look in the mirror to work on the monkey's scratching motions and the rabbit's twitching and head moving. As you work, remember which hand you use for each character to obtain the most effective movements.

Introduction

What to Say

Storyteller: Children, today I am going to have some puppets help me with a story. Wait right there while I check to see if they are ready to help.

What to Do

Turn away from the children to put on the monkey and rabbit. Turn back toward the audience with the puppets hidden behind your back.

The Story

Now, once a monkey . . . and a rabbit . . . were sitting together near the edge of the river.

Make the monkey puppet scamper out from behind your back in the pause right after you say the word "monkey." Then have the rabbit puppet hop out from behind your back during the pause following the word "rabbit."

The monkey was busy scratching himself. First he scratched his arm, then his chin, then the top of his head. He was always scratching!

In this part, have the monkey demonstrate by scratching all the places you mention as you mention them. You may alter the description to reflect places that your monkey puppet can easily and effectively scratch. During this scene, the rabbit watches the monkey.

The rabbit was just as busy moving as the monkey. The rabbit was constantly checking to see if danger was near. She sniffed the air, and this made her nose wriggle and twitch. She moved her head from side to side, and this made her ears flop about. She was always watching for danger!

Monkey watches and Rabbit moves as you describe her movements. Make the sniffing and nose wriggling exaggerated so the audience can easily see them. You may add and describe other movements your rabbit can do well that a rabbit might do while watching for danger.

Monkey: Will you stop turning your head and flopping your ears and wriggling your nose! You are driving me crazy! What a bad habit you have!

The monkey looks straight at the rabbit and moves emphatically as he speaks. You may wish to make him scratch once or twice for emphasis.

Rabbit: Me! What about you? You scratch and scratch and scratch. You are never still. You are driving me crazy! What a bad habit *you* have!

The rabbit looks right at the monkey, who jumps back a bit in astonishment at the rabbit's words.

Monkey: Oh, I can stop scratching if I want to.

Monkey nods his head, being a bit obvious in his care not to scratch. Perhaps he could clap his hands together and hold them there.

Rabbit: Well, *I* can stop moving my head if *I* want to.

The rabbit looks straight at the monkey and gives an emphatic hop, keeping her head and nose still.

Storyteller: They argued for a long time, until at last the monkey made a suggestion for a contest.

Look from one animal to the other, and then out to the audience.

Monkey: This contest will show which one of us is strong enough to really break a bad habit. I say that I will keep very still until the sun goes down. And I'll bet you are turning your head and wriggling your nose before the sun gets low enough in the sky to go behind that tree over there.

Monkey points to himself as he talks about keeping still, points to Rabbit as he talks about how soon she will be moving, and points off toward the audience to show the location of the imaginary tree.

Rabbit: I am sure that I can keep still longer than you can. Let's begin the contest!

Rabbit turns slightly to face Monkey, nods "yes," and then is perfectly still.

Monkey: All right. Begin!

Monkey turns slightly to face Rabbit, nods "yes," and then is perfectly still.

Storyteller: As you can see, Monkey and Rabbit kept perfectly still . . . for a very short time.

Look first at Monkey, then at Rabbit, and then at the audience. Emphasize the phrase "for a very short time."

But it seemed like a verrrry lonnng time to Monkey and Rabbit.

Nod your head "yes" as you continue to look at the audience.

Never had Monkey's skin felt so itchy in so many places.	**Look down at Monkey.**
Never had Rabbit felt so fearful that danger was near.	**Look down at Rabbit.**
Monkey felt that if he could not at least scratch one itching ear, he would die.	**Look back at Monkey.**
Rabbit felt that if she could not turn her head soon to look for the danger she was sure was coming, she would die. Finally, she spoke.	**Look at Rabbit.**
Rabbit: Of course, I am fine being perfectly still, Monkey, but I am beginning to feel bored. The sun is still high in the sky, so we have a long time left together. Let's tell stories to pass the time.	**Rabbit moves slightly to show she is talking, but she is careful not to make the moves of her "bad habit."**
Monkey: All right.	**Monkey nods "yes."**
Storyteller: The monkey suspected the rabbit was going to trick him, so he decided to watch carefully.	**Look at the audience and speak this as an aside just to them.**
Rabbit: This is a story of a time, just last week, when I was very near this river.	**Rabbit turns her head to look at the imaginary river on your right. Monkey remains still, watching Rabbit.**
I heard a noise behind me, and quickly I turned to look.	**Rabbit turns her head and body around to look behind her.**
Then I heard a noise on my left and turned to look. I was afraid the sound came from a lion sneaking up to eat me, so I sniffed the air to see.	**Rabbit turns back around and looks to her left. Then she wriggles her nose.**
Storyteller: Monkey quickly caught on to Rabbit's trick.	**Say this with delight in your voice.**
Monkey: Now it's *my* turn to tell a story! Last week I was walking near the village, and a group of children started throwing coconuts at me.	**Monkey jumps up and down with excitement and speaks very fast.**
One coconut hit me here.	**Monkey scratches his ear.**
Another coconut hit me here.	**Monkey scratches his chest.**
One hit me here.	**Monkey scratches the back of his head.**
Storyteller: Rabbit began to laugh. She laughed so hard that Monkey couldn't help it, and he laughed, too.	**Say these lines with laughter in your own voice. Monkey and Rabbit laugh together and pat each other on the back.**
Each one knew why the other was telling the story that way.	**Say this in a very knowing tone, implying that the children understand, too. If your audience is very young and may not understand, add a line of explanation here, such as: "Monkey knew Rabbit told the story to give an excuse to move her head and wriggle her nose, and Rabbit knew Monkey just told the story so he could scratch without losing the contest!"**
Rabbit: Monkey, I have not lost our contest!	**Rabbit shakes her head "no" at Monkey.**
Monkey: We were both just telling our stories as they should be told.	**This is spoken in a tongue-in-cheek tone.**

Rabbit: I must admit, it is very hard to break a bad habit.

Through this conversation, the puppet who is talking should move a little. The one who is listening should be still after turning slightly toward the speaker. Keep your different voices for the different characters in mind as they speak.

Monkey: It **is** very hard to break a bad habit. . . . I give up!

Monkey begins scratching again.

Rabbit: I give up, too.

Rabbit wriggles her nose and moves her head from side to side, causing her ears to flop.

Storyteller: So the rabbit's nose wriggled, her head turned from side to side, and her ears flopped. The monkey scratched his skin as often as it itched.

The animals keep moving. Look at each one as you describe their actions.

And from that day to this no monkey or rabbit has kept still for very long.

Still scratching and wriggling, Monkey and Rabbit scurry and hop out of sight behind your back.

And that's the story from West Africa about bad habits.

Rabbit and Monkey come back out and take a bow before you put them away in their bag.

Two Versions of the Story

Carpenter, Frances. *African Wonder Tales*, "Who Can Break a Bad Habit?" Illustrated by Joseph Escourido. New York: Doubleday, 1963.

MacDonald, Margaret Read. *Twenty Tellable Tales*, "How to Break a Bad Habit." Illustrated by Roxane Murphy. Bronx, NY: Wilson, 1986.

THE THREE BILLY GOATS GRUFF
Norwegian

Characters/Themes: Families, Food, Scary Creatures

Ages: 3 to 8. The older children usually already know the story well and enjoy saying the lines with you and watching the puppets act out the story.

Puppets Needed: Finger puppets for Troll, Biggest Billy Goat Gruff, Medium-size Billy Goat Gruff, and Smallest Billy Goat Gruff are used. The instructions and information with this script assume that you are using four finger puppets to act out the story. If you wish to do a more simple version, you may tell the story using only a troll puppet. Instructions for this style are listed below under "Alternative Method".

Voices: The troll's voice should carry well, being slightly louder than the first two goats but not quite as loud as the Biggest Billy Goat Gruff's. Try adding a nasal tone to the troll's voice, as that will make him sound sly and sneaky and distinguish him from the Biggest Billy Goat Gruff's voice.

The three goats could simply have high, medium, and low/loud voices. To add more character, think carefully about how each goat is feeling as he crosses the bridge. Perhaps the littlest one could be an intellectual with a problem. He would then present the solution (eat my brother instead) with great satisfaction once he thought of it. The middle goat could have a timid tone to his voice, being truly frightened of the troll and shaking as he delivers his lines. The biggest goat, of course, is not afraid at all and sounds very confident as well as very powerful whenever he speaks.

The Biggest Billy Goat Gruff confronts the Troll on a bridge made of your hands.

Instructions: This story, too, is fairly easy to learn and to tell because there is repetition both in the events that occur and the lines that are spoken. As you learn this story, say it aloud from the very beginning and practice your different voices. Be sure to practice with your puppets in front of a mirror once or twice before performing for the children.

Alternative Method: A simpler way to act out this story is to use only a troll hand puppet, hiding the puppet behind your back and bringing him out when the troll is present in the story. This style is very similar to the way "The Little Red Hen and the Grain of Wheat" is presented in this book. You play the parts of the narrator and the goats. The troll puppet talks to you as if you are the goat to whom he is speaking, and you respond as each different goat character.

The only tricky action to portray is the fight at the end between the troll and the Biggest Billy Goat Gruff. Shorten those lines to say, "So the troll flew at the billy goat. And the billy goat flew at the troll, lifted him up onto his horns, and threw him into the river where he landed with a big . . . *splash*!" As you say the lines, move the troll back and forth first and then lift the troll high into the air with a flourish, and swoop him down to hide behind your back once more as you say the word "splash."

Introduction

What to Say

It's time for a story that some puppets are going to help me tell you. Wait right there while I see if they are ready to help.

What to Do

Turn your back on the children to put on the finger puppets. Put the troll on your left thumb, facing to your right. All the goats go on your right hand, facing left. (If you are left-handed, you may find you need to reverse these directions.) Put the small and middle-sized goats on your index and middle fingers, respectively, and put the biggest goat on your thumb. Check to be sure they are facing the proper direction. (As you can imagine, it's embarrassing to have the troll on backwards, causing him to pop up facing away from the goat he is confronting.) After you have all the puppets on, turn to face the children while hiding both of your hands behind your back.

The Story

Once upon a time there were three billy goats, and the name of all three was Gruff. Now these three billy goats lived on a bare piece of land.

With your head, look to your right and nod to indicate that that is where the goats are now living on the bare land.

They had eaten every bush, every flower, and finally every blade of grass, so they were very hungry.

Nearby there was a beautiful hillside, filled with flowers and trees and sweet green grass.

Look to your left to show that the hillside is on that side.

But... to get to that hillside, there was a bridge over which they had to cross.

Bring your left arm out with your elbow bent so that your hand is slightly above waist high and near the center of your body. Your fingers should be out straight to indicate the bridge, while the troll on your thumb is hidden behind the palm of your hand.

And underneath the bridge lived a great, ugly troll, with eyes as big as saucers and a nose as long as a poker.

As you say the line about the troll with great drama, have the troll pop up from behind the bridge, laugh an evil laugh as he looks around, and hide again behind the bridge. Keep this arm in place for the remainder of the story.

First it was the turn of the Smallest Billy Goat Gruff to cross the bridge.

Bring your right arm out with the elbow bent so that your right hand is level with, and near to, your left. Your fist should be closed, with only your index finger up showing the smallest goat. The other two goats should not be very visible to the audience. It may be impossible to keep every bit of the other two goats hidden, so just do your best. The children's attention will be on the one that is totally visible and acting his part in the story, and so they will be willing to ignore a glimpse of the other goats hiding in your hand.

Trip trap, trip trap, trip trap went the bridge. When the Smallest Billy goat Gruff was almost to the center of the bridge, up jumped they ugly troll!

Make the puppet action coincide with your words, having the troll pop out just as you say, "Up jumped the ugly troll!"

Troll: Who's that tripping over my bridge?

As the goat and the troll are face to face, have the one who is talking move a little to indicate he is speaking.

Smallest Billy Goat Gruff: Oh, it is just me, the Smallest Billy Goat Gruff, and I am on my way up the hillside to eat grass and get fat.

The goat looks first at the troll and then around the troll toward the imaginary hillside.

Troll: Oh no you're not! I'm coming to gobble you up!

Troll moves from side to side to indicate "no."

Smallest Billy Goat Gruff: Oh, don't eat me! Wait for my brother. He's much bigger and fatter than I, and he'll make a better meal for you.

Pause here, as if thinking what to do, and then present the little goat's idea about his brother.

Troll: Bigger, you say?

Speak slowly and thoughtfully.

Smallest Billy Goat Gruff: Yes, much bigger.

Speak emphatically.

79

Troll: Fatter, you say?

Speak even more slowly and thoughtfully.

Smallest Billy Goat Gruff: Yes, much fatter.

Speak enthusiastically.

Troll: All right. I will wait. But you be on your way!

After a moment's hesitation, the troll decides, and then he disappears behind your palm again.

Storyteller: So the Smallest Billy Goat Gruff went on across the bridge and up onto the beautiful hillside where he began to eat the sweet green grass.

Have the goat walk across the bridge and up your arm to your left shoulder where he pantomimes eating grass for a moment. Then, swiftly bring your hand behind your back again to hide the smallest goat in your fist and bring up the medium-size goat.

Then it was the turn of the Medium-size Billy Goat Gruff to cross the bridge. Trip trap, trip trap, trip trap went the bridge, a little louder this time.

Walk the medium-size goat out to the bridge, moving him in time with your trip trap sounds.

Troll: Who's that tripping over my bridge?

Troll pops up from behind your palm as he speaks. Goat jumps back in fright and begins shaking.

Medium-Size Billy Goat Gruff: Oh, it is just me, the Medium-size Billy Goat Gruff, and I am on my way up the hillside to eat grass and get fat.

This goat is really frightened, and his voice shakes as he replies.

Troll: Well, I've been waiting for you! I'm coming to . . . gobble you up!

Pause before the phrase "gobble you up" to build suspense.

Medium-Size Billy Goat Gruff: Oh, d-d-d-don't eat me! Wait for my brother. He's much b-b-b-bigger and fatter than I, and he'll make a better meal for you.

The goat's voice still trembles, and he stutters some as he answers.

Troll: Bigger, you say?

Sound sly.

Medium-Size Billy Goat Gruff: Oh yes, much b-b-bigger.

Still frightened.

Troll: Fatter, you say?

Sound delighted.

Medium-Size Billy Goat Gruff: Oh yes, much fatter.

Nods head "yes."

Troll: All right. I will wait. But you be on your way!

Troll disappears behind your palm again.

Storyteller: So the Medium-size Billy Goat Gruff went on across the bridge and up onto the beautiful hillside where he began to eat the sweet green grass with his brother.

The medium-size goat walks on across the bridge and up your left arm to your shoulder. If it's not too difficult, bring out the smallest goat and pantomime the two goats eating grass together. Then swiftly move your arm back behind you to hide them both in your fist and bring up the biggest goat.

Then it was the turn of the Biggest Billy Goat Gruff to cross the bridge. *Trip trap, trip trap, trip trap* went the Biggest Billy Goat Gruff, and he was so heavy that the bridge creaked and groaned under his weight.

This goat stomps slowly and heavily out from behind your back, moving in time with the trip trap sounds.

Troll: Who's that tripping over my bridge?

The troll pops up from behind the "bridge" (your palm) to confront the goat in a loud voice.

Biggest Billy Goat Gruff: It is I, the Biggest Billy Goat Gruff, and I'm on my way up the hillside to eat grass and get fat.

Sound just as forceful as the troll, and a bit louder.

Storyteller: And his voice was even bigger and louder than the troll's.

Say this with surprise in your voice as an aside to the audience.

Troll: Oh no you're not! I've been waiting for you . . . and I'm coming to gobble you up!

Speak forcefully.

Biggest Billy Goat Gruff: Well, come ahead. I'm not afraid of you.

Speak in the same loud, confident, forceful voice used earlier.

Storyteller: And so the billy goat flew at the troll. And the troll flew at the billy goat. They fought for a long time. Sometimes the billy goat got tired. Sometimes the troll got tired. But on they fought.

Pantomime the fight. Your hands are near each other, and because the two characters are on your thumbs, there is lots of potential for action. Show near misses, and at times each character lays over on his side and pants with fatigue for a second as you describe their fight.

At last, the billy goat lifted the troll up on his horns and threw him into the river where he landed with a big *splash!* And the troll floated away down the river and was never seen again.

The goat tosses the troll high into the air, and when the troll comes back down, float him out of sight behind your back as you say the final sentence slowly and with a great deal of satisfaction in your voice.

As for the Biggest Billy Goat Gruff, he went on across the bridge and up onto the hillside to join his brothers in eating the sweet green grass. As far as I know, they are still there, eating grass and getting very *fat.*

When the biggest goat gets to your shoulder, bring out the other two and show the three brothers eating together there for a second.

Snip snap snout
This tale's told out.

Then, as you end the story, have the three goats turn to the audience, take a quick bow, and then walk behind your back.

THE THREE LITTLE PIGS
English

Characters/Themes: Pigs, Wolves

Ages: 2 to 5

Puppets and Props Needed: You will need a hand puppet wolf and one hand puppet pig. The instructions that follow assume that you are using one pig to play the parts of all three little pigs. The straw, sticks, bricks, and houses in this telling are imaginary. If possible, sit in a chair with arms as you tell the story. The arms provide places for imaginary building supplies and completed houses to be located.

You could also develop this story using only a hand puppet wolf. Read the script "The Little Red Hen and the Grain of Wheat" to get an idea of how a story with more than one character may be told by a storyteller using a single puppet.

Voices and Characterization: The wolf's voice needs to be gruff and loud but not too scary for the age group in the audience.

Since you are using one pig puppet to represent all three little pigs, your presentation will be more effective if you can develop three distinct voices and personalities for the three pigs. Some suggestions are included here. Read them and try them out, modifying them to suit the characters you are most comfortable portraying.

The first pig might be the oldest sibling—a brash, know-it-all type. He doesn't want to be bothered spending too much effort or time on his house so he is satisfied when he finds straw for his building material. His voice could be loud, abrupt, and full of boasting.

The second pig, the middle child, is more happy-go-lucky, singing as she enters and charmed with the audience's idea of using sticks to build her house. Her voice is lighter, bubbling, and full of delight.

The third and youngest pig could be somewhat of a nerd—a careful, scientific type who plans well and is willing to work. His voice might have a deliberate, calculating quality. To make the third pig's voice more distinct, consider having him sound a bit like a pig with a cold in his nose.

Instructions: This story is another easy one to learn, because similar events and lines are repeated. It is challenging to tell with puppets because it is most effective if you can create very different voices for the three pigs and the wolf.

This script assumes you are telling this story to a group already familiar with the tale. It allows for audience participation opportunities that delight the children. The pigs draw the children's participation by asking them for advice in solving their housing problems, and the wolf is always asking, "Has anyone seen a little pig around here?" Children end up playing the parts of those who provide sticks and bricks for the pigs to build their houses. The children also assist in creating dramatic suspense as they help the wolf huff and puff and blow at the pigs' houses.

Introduction

What to Say

Storyteller: Today, I am going to need a lot of help in telling a story. I have brought some helpers with me. Just a minute while I see if they are ready.

During the story, I may ask some of you to help, too. Today I am going to tell you a story that some of you already know. It is the story of "The Three Little Pigs."

What to Do

Turn your back on the children to put on the puppets. If you are right-handed you probably will want to wear the pig on your right hand, as the pig has the most to do. Turn back quickly to face the children with your hands behind your back.

It is good to acknowledge that some children will know the story already. Otherwise, they may interrupt you to tell you they do.

The Story

Storyteller: All of you who know the story already probably remember that it begins like this . . .

One day, mother pig called all three of her little pigs

Look at the children and speak in a motherly tone.

to her and said, "Children, you are old enough now to go out and make your own way in the world. Be careful, build your houses well, and be sure to come home for visits."

"All right, Mama, we will," replied the three little pigs.

And the oldest pig, who liked to be first in everything, set off first to see the world.	As you say this, have the pig puppet walk out from behind your back.
First Pig: Yeah! I'm out in the world at last. And I'm ready to build my house. I want to build it fast because I want lots of time to have adventures! Wonder what I could use	He speaks with bold confidence, looking around and scratching his head as he wonders what building material to use.
Storyteller: I have some straw here you could use.	You and the pig look at each other as you offer him some imaginary straw, indicating with a gesture of your head that it's in a pile to your left.
First Pig: Hey, that will be great. I can build a house in no time with straw.	The pig looks at storyteller and then at pile of imaginary straw.
This job is so simple! I'll have this house built in no time. It's looking really good!	As the pig picks up piles of imaginary straw from the left arm of your chair and piles them up around the right arm of your chair, he continues to boast.
There, my house is finished.	The pig looks at the house from all sides.
I think I'll go inside and take a rest before I go off on my adventures.	The pig goes inside the house and lies down on the arm of the chair so that his eyes are hidden from the audience. He snores loudly once or twice.
Wolf: Hmmmm. I smell pig. I'm not sure where it is, but I know it's around here somewhere.	Wolf enters from the left, looking away from the pig and sniffing. He keeps looking around and sniffing loudly. Finally he turns to face the pig and jumps back in astonishment.
Whoa. I have never seen that straw house before. I'll bet the pig is inside. I'll go see.	Wolf slowly approaches the imaginary house, sniffing all the while.
Yes, I smell pig for sure!	The wolf is standing very near to the pig.
Little pig, little pig, let me come in.	The wolf speaks loudly and gruffly. The pig wakes up, startled, and sits up.
First Pig: Oh, no. Not by the hair of my chinny chin chin.	The pig stands up and faces the wolf, trembling and shouting through the imaginary straw wall.
Wolf: Well, then, I'll huff . . .	He breathes in a big breath and blows it toward the pig, who trembles.
and I'll puff . . .	He breathes in another big breath, blowing it toward the pig who trembles more violently.
and I'll blooowwww your house in.	Wolf blows furiously toward the pig, and the pig floats up and away with the force of the air. Bring the pig quickly down again, hiding it out of sight on your right side.
Say, where did that pig go? I'll follow my nose and find him!	Sniffing loudly, the wolf runs around behind your left side out of sight.

83

Storyteller: And the wolf ate up the first little pig.

Say this line using a matter-of-fact tone.

Next came the second little pig, out to seek her fortune.

The second pig—really the same pig puppet—comes bouncing happily out from behind your back, singing to herself.

Second Pig: Oh, the world is so much fun. But I had better build a house before night falls. Wonder what I could use . . . .

She stops and pats her cheek as she wonders what to use to build her house.

Do you have any ideas about what I might use to build a house?

She looks toward the children. When you ask the audience, several responses are possible.

If they suggest materials besides sticks, have the pig reject the ideas as positively as you can, using comments like "A stone house would be very nice, but the stones around here are too heavy for me to lift." Try to keep the ideas coming until someone thinks of sticks. If no one does, you must eventually have the pig think of it herself.

If the response is silence, ask them again in a slightly different way, perhaps having the pig ask something like, "Have you ever built a house before? What did you use?" If the children remain silent, you can handle this one like the first, by supplying the idea yourself.

Second Pig: Sticks! What a wonderful idea! Sticks will be perfect for building my house.

If a child has volunteered the sticks, the pig might ask the child to bring them to her or to carefully toss the sticks up to the front of the room. She could invite all the children to participate by tossing imaginary sticks to the front of the room as she pretends to catch them. Once the pig has the sticks, she begins to pile them up around the right arm of your chair, cheerfully humming a tune as she works.

The wolf huffs and puffs and blows away the little pig's imaginary house, and the little pig as well.

Oh, what a wonderful house.

The pig looks at the house from all sides.

It's finished at last, and I'm tired from all that work.

She goes inside the house and lies down on the right arm of your chair. She may wish to dust off the spot a little before lying down with her head curled away from the audience to hide her eyes. She gives a big sigh and snores softly.

Wolf: Hmmmm. I smell pig. Have any of you seen a pig around here?

The wolf enters from the left, looking away from the pig and sniffing. He keeps looking around and sniffing loudly. If the children give him advice about where the pig is, he bumbles around looking in the wrong directions. Finally he turns to face the pig and jumps back in astonishment.

Whoa. I have never seen that stick house before. I'll bet the pig is inside. I'll go see.

Wolf slowly approaches the house, sniffing all the while.

Yes, I smell pig for sure! Little pig, little pig, let me come in.

The wolf speaks in a loud, gruff voice. The pig wakes up, startled, and sits up.

Second Pig: Oh, no. Not by the hair of my chinny chin chin.

She stands up and faces the wolf, shouting.

Wolf: Well, then, I'll huff . . .

He breathes in a big breath and blows it toward the pig, who trembles.

and I'll puff . . .

He breathes in another big breath, blowing it toward the pig, who trembles more violently.

and I'll blooowwww your house in. Boys and girls, help me blow.

Wolf asks the children to help him blow. With the children, the wolf blows furiously toward the pig, and the pig quickly floats up and away to the right, then down again out of sight behind your back on the right side.

Wolf: Come back here, pig!

Wolf runs off around your left side and out of sight.

Storyteller: And the wolf ate up the second little pig.

Say this using a matter-of-fact tone.

Now the third little pig leaves home.

Bring the pig puppet out from behind your back once more.

Third Pig: Now I know the first thing I should do is build a house. I want a house that is very strong because I know a wolf lives around here, and that wolf eats little pigs. I must find something to build my house with right away.

Remember to make this third pig sound like an intellectual with a cold.

Say, do you have any ideas about something strong I could use to build my house?

The pig turns to the audience. If the children make suggestions, deal with them as you did for the second little pig. When someone suggests bricks, have that child bring them to the pig rather than throw them. Bricks flying through the air could be very danger-ous! An alternative would be to find an imaginary brick pile nearby.

This pile of bricks will be just fine. This is hard work, but my house will be very strong. Let's see . . . I think I'll make a chimney right around here.

Oh, what a strong and sturdy house. I am sure this house will protect me from the wolf.

It's finished at last, and I'm tired from all that work. I think I'll go into my brand new house and take a nap where I will be safe and comfortable.

Wolf: Hmmmm. I smell pig. Have any of you seen a pig around here?

Whoa. I have never seen that brick house before. I'll bet the pig is inside. I'll go see.

Yes, I smell pig for sure! Little pig, little pig, let me come in.

Third Pig: Oh, no. Not by the hair of my chinny chin chin.

Wolf: Well, then, I'll huff . . .

and I'll puff . . .

and I'll blooowwww your house in. Boys and girls, help me blow.

Let's try again . . .

Whew, that house is strong.

One . . . two . . . three . . . blow!

Everyone help. If we blow as hard as we can, I know we can do it. All together now.

I cannot blow this brick house in, even with your help. I will have to think of a new plan.

Look at that chimney! I will climb down that chimney and catch the little pig!

Third Pig: If that wolf is coming down the chimney, I'd better get a pot of boiling water onto my fire!

There, now I am ready for that wolf!

The pig mumbles to himself as he works. Be sure to remember where your imaginary chimney is located, as you will need to know when the wolf is ready to come down the chimney.

The pig looks at the house from all sides.

The pig goes inside the house and lies down on the right arm of your chair. He turns and wiggles a bit before setting down to sleep. He has a funny, nasal snore to go with his voice.

He enters from the left, looking away from the pig and sniffing. If the children give him advice about where the pig is, he bumbles around looking in the wrong directions. Finally he turns to face the pig and jumps back in astonishment.

Wolf slowly approaches the house, sniffing all the while.

The pig wakes up, startled, and sits up.

Stands up and faces the wolf, shouting.

He breathes in a big breath and blows it toward the pig, who stands firm.

He breathes in another big breath, blowing it toward the pig, who still stands firm.
Wolf asks the children to help him blow. With the children, the wolf blows furiously toward the pig, the pig stands firm. The wolf tries again, but still the pig doesn't move. The wolf falls over with the effort of his huffing and puffing. When he has rested a moment, he asks the children to blow their hardest this one last time. Everyone does, and the wolf falls over again, panting. The pig is very still.

Wolf thoughtfully walks around the outside of the house, looking it over very carefully, until he spots the chimney!

He stops and focuses his attention on the chimney.

Inside his house, the pig hears the wolf and goes into action.

Pig pantomimes setting up pot of boiling water.

86

Wolf: Ready or not, here I come . . . up onto the roof and dooowwwwn the chimney! AAAAAHHHHHHhhhhhhhhhhhhhhhssssssssssss!!	The wolf pantomimes the actions as he describes them. The wolf lands on the arm of the chair where the third pig has placed his imaginary pot.
Third Pig: Well, that's the end of that wolf—boiled as soup for my supper.	The pig takes the wolf puppet off your hand and slings the wolf over his shoulder.
And I am safe!	He speaks his final line in a matter-of-fact tone as he carries the wolf off behind your back to the right.

THE LITTLE POT
Swedish

Characters/Themes: Imagination, Surprises

Ages: 5 to 8

Puppet Needed: Any inanimate object brought to life before an audience is a puppet, and you will bring a cooking pot to life in telling this tale. In addition to the pot and lid, you'll need a bag in which to keep the pot and a scouring rag to polish the pot.

If you enjoy garage sales and thrift stores, you may wish to keep your eyes open for just the right pot to use in telling this tale. The original story describes it as a little, old iron pot with three short legs and a big round handle. Any easy-to-handle cooking pot with a lid, borrowed from your kitchen, will be fine. Just alter the description of the pot as you tell the story.

You may use any cloth bag, even a pillowcase, as the bag to hold the pot. Describing your bag as the one the stranger uses to carry the pot, and drawing the pot out slowly when the stranger offers the pot to the old man in exchange for the cow, can add a strong dramatic moment to your version of the tale. The scouring rag can be any kind of cloth—from an old dish towel to a bandana handkerchief.

Voices and Characterization: Develop a different voice for the pot than you use for the other characters in the story. Think of the pot as young and mischievous, with a light and lighthearted voice. The rich man and his wife are in the prime of their lives, greedy and used to having their own way. The poor old couple are in their seventies. Try wrapping your bottom lip around your teeth to assist you in speaking slowly and sounding old.

Instruction: A childlike sense of play will help you in the effective use of your pot as a puppet in this story. Observe children at play with their dolls, action figures, or even sticks. Children use all these objects as if they were alive, giving them voices and moving them to act out events. You will be doing a similar thing with your pot, acting as if it is alive with a voice and mind of its own.

Experiment with movements for your pot in front of a mirror. During the story, the pot skips, hops, and bounces down the road.

The Story

Once, in the far-off Northland, there lived a man and his wife who were very old and very poor. For many years they had worked hard for a rich man. The rich man had paid them little, even though he was very rich, with a big house and barn, thousands of acres of farmland, and more. The rich man was greedy and stingy and paid them only enough to get by, not enough to save for their future.

When the old couple could no longer work, they soon had nothing in their house to eat. They had but one thing left, a fine cow. Now she gave them milk, and they used that to make butter and cheese, so they hated to sell her. Finally, they had nothing left to feed the cow, and they decided they must sell her.

As the old man was preparing to take the cow to market, he asked his wife, "What do you think our cow is worth?"

His wife answered, "She's such a fine cow, I think she is worth at least eighty dollars."

"All right, dear. I will sell her for eighty dollars," he agreed.

They got up very early the next morning, and the man started to the market, leading the cow behind him. The market was a long way off, and it was the middle of the afternoon before he finally could see the market way off in the distance. Just as he could see the market, he saw a strange man coming toward him up the road.

"Where are you going with that cow?" asked the stranger.

The old man said, "To the market to sell her."

"How much do you expect to get for her?" asked the stranger.

"Seeing that she is an unusually fine cow, I expect to get eighty dollars."

"Well, I haven't eighty dollars, but I have something that is worth eighty dollars, which I will give you for her."

What to Say

The stranger reached into an old-looking bag with many patches and pulled out a pot—a plain, ordinary, silver-colored cooking pot with two black handles.

The old man looked at it in astonishment for a minute and said, "You don't think I am so foolish as to give you my cow for that old silver pot!"

Just then, the pot spoke up.

"Take me! Take me!"

"Well!" thought the man, "if the little pot can talk like that, I'd better take it."

Giving the stranger the cow, the old man put the pot back into its bag and started home.

What to Do

As you speak these lines, bring up the bag that has been sitting beside your chair. Pantomime the actions as they are told by the narrator, acting as if you are the stranger with the pot. Make sure you describe your bag and pot, not the items described here.

Say this with astonishment.

Say this in a matter-of-fact tone.

As you enthusiastically speak for the pot, move the pot as if it is speaking enthusiastically. You might tip it front to back or side to side, clanking the lid a bit as you do so. You might want to make it jump up and down on your lap. Do whatever action works best for your pot's shape.

Put your pot back into its bag and swing the bag over your shoulder for the journey home.

The journey was as long going as it had been coming, so it grew dark long before he arrived. Along the way, the old man had much time to think of the eighty dollars he had promised his wife he would get for the cow. He walked more and more slowly as he thought of what she might say about his bargain.

You may remain seated and just describe the trip.

When he finally arrived at home, he took the pot straight to the cowshed, took it out of the bag, and set it down in the straw right where the cow used to stand.

Take the pot out of the bag and set it near you on a table or chair in clear view of the audience. (If you put the pot on the floor where they can't see it, they will be distracted straining to see it. Plan ahead of time where to place the pot so it will be easy for the audience to see.)

Then he went into the house. His wife got him some supper, and after he had eaten it, she asked, "Well, husband, did you get a good price for the cow?"

"W-e-e-l-l-l, come see what I got for her."

Speak in the husband's voice; it is not necessary to say who is talking.

They lit the lantern and went down to the cowshed. Holding the lantern up high, he told her to look into the stall. At first she could see nothing, but when her eyes became accustomed to the dusk of the place, she saw the old silver pot with two black handles sitting there in the straw. When she realized what it was, she turned to her husband and asked, "Do you mean to tell me that's what you got for our cow?"

Use the storyteller's voice for most of this, but speak in the wife's voice when she speaks. She sounds astonished and angry.

"Yes, this is what I got for her."

Speak in the husband's voice. Pick up the pot from the table and hold it on your lap.

"Well! You are more foolish than I thought you were, husband!"

Just then, the little pot said, "Take me into the house and scour me up bright and put me on the fire!"

As the pot speaks, again move it as if it were speaking enthusiastically.

"My!" exclaimed the old woman. "If that old pot can talk, I think we had better do as it says."

So they took the pot into the house, and the next morning the old wife got out the scouring cloth and polished up the pot.

As you say this, rub the pot with the cloth taken from the pot's bag.

She put it on the fire.

Pantomime this as you speak by setting the pot deliberately down on your lap. Hold it still until it speaks.

As soon as it began to get hot, the pot spoke up, "I skip! I skip!"

Move the pot enthusiastically to show it is speaking.

"Where do you skip?" cried the old woman.

Look at the pot as you ask the question.

"Oh, I skip to the house of the rich man!" And giving a big jump, the little pot went out through the window and down the hard road.

As you pantomime the pot's journey, try to show as many of the actions as you can. Begin with a big jump. The pot may run by moving side to side as well as quickly forward, clanging its lid as it runs. Use your free hand to clang the lid. Give it a bit of a zigzag course so that it will have farther to go.

In a minute it was at the rich man's house, and it jumped right through the window and landed on the table.

Have the pot finish its journey by jumping back on your lap, clamping its lid shut, and being still until it speaks again.

That morning the rich man's wife was making a fine pudding, and she had around her all the things that were to go into it: sugar, and flour, and butter, and raisins, and nuts, and more. She was so pleased when the little pot landed on her table. She called out, "Husband, see how bright and clean this little pot is. It is just the thing to put my pudding in!"

Look around you as you speak of the fine ingredients she'll be using for the pudding.

She went on mixing her pudding. When she had finished, she put it into the little pot. As soon as she had it all in, the pot cried out, "I skip! I skip!"

Open the pot's lid as you say "she put it into the little pot." Make the pot's lid clatter as it speaks.

"Well, where do you skip?" asked the rich woman in astonishment.

Look at the pot.

But the little pot was gone without an answer. With one leap, it jumped out the window and bumped down the road until it was back at the house of the poor man and his wife.,

Pantomime these actions of the pot as you describe them with words. Make it leap and run away from you in a zigzag course, landing back on your lap again as it arrives at the poor couple's house.

The old woman, busy at her work, heard a racket behind her. When she looked around, she saw the little pot standing on the kitchen table.

Look at the pot in surprise.

When she saw what was in it, she called, "Husband! The pot has come back, and see what a fine pudding it has brought us!"

Lift the lid and look into the pot yourself, as if you are the old woman.

Then she set the pot over the fire, and they had the finest pudding they ever ate. It lasted two or three days.

Pantomime setting the pot to one side, over the fire.

When they finished the pudding, the woman scoured up the pot again until it shone and put it on the fire again.

Use your scouring rag to polish the pot and then set it back on the fire.

As soon as it began to get hot, the pot spoke up, "I skip! I skip!"

Remember to move the pot's lid slightly as it talks, to show us it's alive.

"Dear me, where do you skip this time?" asked the old woman.

Look at the pot.

"Oh, I skip to the *barn* of the rich man!"

As you speak for it, make the pot jump up and down with excitement. Emphasize the word "barn."

The little pot jumped out into the middle of the road and thumped down the road until it reached the barn of the rich man and stopped in the middle of the big floor.

Pantomime the actions of the journey with the pot as you describe them. When it stops in the middle of the barn floor, place it back on your lap and put the lid down with a flourish.

That morning, the rich man's servants were threshing his wheat. One of them spied the shiny pot. "Look at this pot! I wonder how it got here! Well, no matter how it came, it is a good thing to put some of this wheat into."

Think of the servants as young, strong men as you speak for them.

So the men took out their shovels and began putting wheat into the pot . . . and putting wheat into the pot . . . and putting wheat into the pot.

Take the lid off the pot and hold it aside as the imaginary wheat is shoveled into it.

But the pot did not get full. They kept on shoveling until they had put every kernel of the rich man's wheat into the pot.

Say this slowly, with your voice full of wonder.

As soon as it was all in, the little pot cried, "I skip! I skip!"

Have the pot dance around as it speaks.

"Oh, where do you skip?" asked the men.

But the pot did not answer. It bounced over the barn floor, out through the open doors, and down the hard road.

Pantomime these actions as you say them, again clanging the lid and bouncing the pot from side to side on a zigzag course.

"Catch it!" cried the men, running after it. But no matter how fast they ran, the little pot bounced and bumped down the road a little faster, and the pot left them far behind. When the pot was out of sight, it bounced back to the house of the poor couple.

At the end of its journey, the pot lands in your lap once more.

The old man, bending over the fire, heard a noise.

Look at the pot.

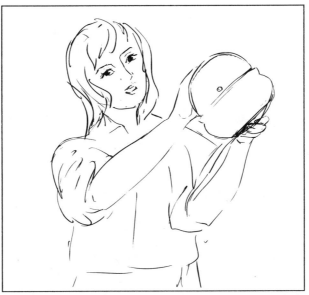

Here is the puppeteer using a real pot as a puppet, pantomiming the action. Bang the pot's lid as it travels, adding sound effects to the journey.

Raising his head, he saw the pot in the middle of the room.

"Look!" he called to his wife. "The pot has come back filled with fine, yellow wheat!"

Lift the lid, look inside the pot, and speak with excitement in your voice.

They began to take the wheat from the pot. No matter how much they took out, the pot seemed to be as full as ever. They kept on until the whole room was nearly filled before the pot was empty.

Gesture to show how much wheat fills the room. Then turn the pot upside down to show it is empty before putting the lid back on.

They had enough wheat to make bread for eight or ten years.

Say this with amazement. Often the children in the audience will exclaim in amazement when they hear this.

The next morning the old couple was resting after their hard day's work storing the rich man's wheat in their cowshed.

Suddenly, the little pot spoke, "I skip! I skip!"

This time, have the speaking pot move more deliberately, as if it is looking right at the old couple.

"Where can you skip to this time?" they asked.

Look at the pot.

"I skip to the house of the rich man!" Then the pot bounced off the table, out the door, and down the road. In a minute the pot was standing on a table, by a window, in the rich man's house.

Show the pot's journey by pantomiming the action as you speak. End with it silent in your lap.

That morning the rich man was counting his treasure, and he had it all spread out on the table before him. There were piles of yellow gold, and great heaps of white silver, and bags and bags of small coins.

Gesture with your hands to show the treasure all around.

The rich man looked up from his counting, saw the little pot standing quietly in front of him, and said, "Why this little pot looks like a fine place to hold some of my money."

Look at the little pot as if you are the rich man.

And so he put money into the pot, and put money into the pot. The little pot did not get full until every bit of the rich man's money was inside.

Pretend to scoop up money and put it into the pot as if you are the rich man.

Then the pot spoke, "I skip! I skip!"

Move the pot as it speaks.

Swiftly, it jumped out the window and into the middle of the road. It bounced and bumped faster than ever until it was back in the kitchen of the poor couple.

Pantomime the journey, ending with a big leap into the kitchen.

As it bounced around the room, it scattered the money in all directions. The old husband and wife gathered it up and hid it all away for safekeeping.

Bounce the pot around in a circle, clanging the lid as you do so. Also move it from side to side as if scattering money.

At last, they had enough money to last them as long as they lived.

Say this slowly, with great satisfaction.

A few days later, while the old couple were rubbing

Rub the pot with the cloth.

the pot and talking of the good fortune it had brought them, suddenly it cried out, "I skip! I skip!"	
"What!" said the old woman and the old man. "Skipping again! Where can it be this time?"	**They sound surprised.**
"Oh, to the house of the rich man!" And bounce and bump went the pot over the hard road and right into the rich man's house.	**Pantomime these actions, finally landing once more on your lap.**
As soon as he saw the pot standing there, the rich man called, "Wife, come here! Here is the pot that stole your pudding, and my wheat, and all our money! Now let us make sure it does not get away this time!" Then he gave a big jump and fell on the pot in the middle of the floor.	**The man sounds quite angry. When he jumps on the pot, open the lid so he can go inside.**
As soon as the pot felt the rich man land, it wriggled and wriggled and opened up until it swallowed the rich man up to his neck!	**Wriggle the pot dramatically throughout this part, clanging the lid against the side.**
Then the pot cried out, "I skip! I skip!"	**Move the pot as it speaks.**
And away it went! The rich man's wife ran after the pot, and the rich man shouted cries of protest, but the pot just went on bouncing and bumping down the road, faster and faster.	**Clang the lid as you make the pot bounce wildly down the road.**
The old man and woman heard the bouncing of the pot and the cries of the rich people as they were passing by. Looking out, they saw the pot carrying the rich man away. "What are you going to do with him?" they shouted.	**Have the pot stop to listen to the poor man and woman, then bounce up and down as it replies.**
"I am going to take him to the North Pole." And away it went over the ice and snow, out of sight into the frozen north.	**As you complete this line, bounce the pot behind your back out of the audience's sight.**
From that day to this, nothing has been heard of the rich man, nor has anything been seen of the little pot. As for the poor man and his wife, they were never hungry again.	**Say this with great satisfaction.**

Story Source: Cox, John Harrington. *Folk Tales of East and West.* Boston: Little, Brown, and Company, 1912. Told by Charles T. Grawn, who learned it as a boy from Swedish folk.

PIERRE

Characters/Themes: Families, Humor, Jungle Beasts, Scary Creatures, Surprises

Ages: 2 to 7

Story Source: Sendak, Maurice. *Pierre: A Cautionary Tale.* New York: Harper & Row, Publishers, 1962.

Puppet Needed: You will need a lion, preferably one with a moving mouth. You can make a very effective lion puppet like the one illustrated here from two boxes that are the same size. (See page 97 for a drawing of the completed lion puppet.) Clean out the boxes, cut the tops off, stand them up side by side, and tape them together securely where they meet at the top. As you can see, the box puppet is just the lion's head. The lion's mane is made from orange and yellow tissue paper strips glued on with extra tacky glue. The rest of his features may be painted on with acrylic paint. Tempera paint tends to peel off and is not satisfactory for a long-lasting puppet.

A small puppet can be made from two small laundry soap boxes rescued from the laundromat. This small size will fit your hand comfortably and be easily visible to a group of up to 30 children. This size will also work for the children to make their own puppets.

If you wish, you can make a large lion from two larger boxes such as breakfast cereal boxes. You may use egg carton cups for eyes on the larger puppet, while painting on the rest of the features. With larger boxes, it is necessary to put straps inside the backs of the boxes, as illustrated on the next page. Make the straps by cutting strips from another cereal box. Staple them in place before taping the boxes together. The strap in the top box is for your fingers, and in the bottom box the strap is for your thumb. These straps allow you to control the movements of the puppet's mouth.

Voice: Tell the story, with the audience participating as described in the introduction. Vary your voice a little for the mother and the father. Mother sounds like a typical housewife, patient but harried. Use a lower voice and a scolding tone for the father, shaking your finger at the audience as Father threatens to send Pierre off to bed. Use a rounder, more booming low voice for the lion. Be careful to modulate the lion's voice to suit the courage of the audience, sounding just scary enough to delight them but not to truly frighten them.

General Information: This script is different than the other story scripts in this section, because the text of this story is not included. It is found in the book *Pierre: A Cautionary Tale* by Maurice Sendak. This book is so popular that you can easily find it in your public library if you are not already familiar with it. The story is such a great success with children and with their parents that it has been included even though you may have to make a special trip to the library or bookstore to get the story text.

Instructions: Do not try this script before you have experienced success using others in this book. This story is more difficult to learn because the text all rhymes and must be memorized. It is well worth the effort, however, as it is very successful with children and their parents as well. Because of its wide age appeal it is a good story to tell to mixed audiences of children and their parents, such as at a pajama storytime or at a group party.

A simpler variation on these instructions would be to read aloud the first part of the story, memorizing only the part near the end when the lion arrives. You will still be able to incorporate all the audience participation outlined in the script if you add "Pierre said . . ." after every other line and refrain from reading the "I don't care" lines so that the children can say them.

If you choose to read aloud rather than memorize the beginning of the story, just put the book down and pick up the bag with the lion in it as you say the line "Now as the night began to fall . . . ." From there, continue the instructions as they are given in this script for the final sequence of events.

Read the entire story before reading the script below. You will need to follow along in the book as you use this script, to see how you can add puppet action to this story. Practice lip syncing with your lion puppet, looking at it in a mirror to see how to move its mouth effectively. Also see how to hold its head so its face is visible to the audience. Help with lip syncing and puppet movement is found in Chapter 8.

Introduction

What to Say

I am going to use a puppet to help me tell the story of a boy named Pierre. Have any of you ever heard this story before?

I see that some of you have. You may put your hands down now. Does anyone remember what Pierre always says in the story?

Yes! Pierre always says "I don't care!" Now as I tell the story I'd like all of you to play the part of Pierre. That means whenever I say "Pierre said . . ." you will say "I don't care." Let's practice that. Pierre said . . .

That's good. As you play the part of Pierre in the story, I want you to think about how Pierre might be feeling as you say his line.

How would you say "I don't care" if you were feeling sleepy?

What about silly?

How would you say it if you were feeling mad?

What to Do

Usually at least a few children raise their hands. If they do, acknowledge them as follows.

Sometimes children shout out the answer. If they raise their hands, call on one to tell the answer.

Pause to let the children respond with "I don't care." If they do not respond, encourage them by saying, "Remember you are playing the part of Pierre." Then repeat "Pierre said . . ." and say the reply with them.

During the next part, where the children are practicing saying the line with different feelings, encourage them by saying "I don't care" with them and using your body as well as your voice to show whatever emotion Pierre might be feeling.

Yawn and stretch and scratch your head as you and the children all say a sleepy "I don't care."

You all giggle and bounce as you say it.

The children always do this one very well, with a lot of power in it.

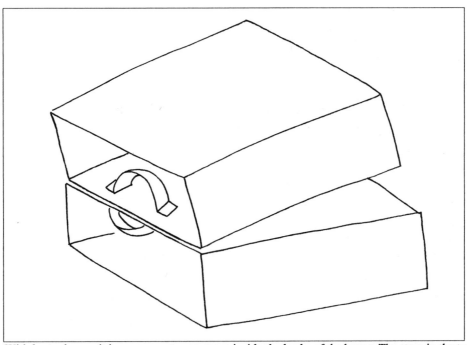

With larger boxes, it is necessary to put straps inside the backs of the boxes. The strap in the top box is for your fingers, and in the bottom box the strap is for your thumb, allowing you to control the movements of the puppet's mouth.

What about bored?	You all look slack-jawed and dull, saying the line very slowly and flatly.
What about frightened?	When you say a frightened "I don't care," you all shiver, hold yourselves tight, and talk in tiny voices.
Now you are ready. Remember, every time I say "Pierre said . . ." you will say what?	The children answer "I don't care."

The Story

Begin to tell the story, saying "Pierre said . . ." after every two rhyming lines, such as:

"What would you like to eat?

Some lovely cream of wheat?

Pierre said. . ."

Pause for the audience to answer. If it seems necessary, encourage the children to participate freely by sometimes joining them, using your body and your voice to show the "I don't care" feelings Pierre might be having.

As you tell the story, relate to the children as if they are all Pierre. For example, as Father enters saying, "Get off your head . . ." shake your finger and look directly at the children as you say those lines in an angry tone.

When Pierre's father and mother leave him home alone, pick up the bag that contains the lion puppet. As you say "Now, as the night began to fall," cautiously peek into the bag, give the children a surprised look, and slowly reach inside with your right hand to put on the puppet. On the next line, swiftly and dramatically bring the lion out of the bag with a flourish and perhaps a "*roar.*"

Continue the narrator's part, having the lion pantomime appropriate actions as you speak. Have the lion say his lines himself while looking at the children, for they are the ones who will be answering him with "I don't care" until he pretends to eat them!

When the lion does eat Pierre, have him lean forward toward the children, opening his mouth wide, snapping it shut in the air, and swallowing Pierre whole with a big gulp. After Pierre is eaten, settle the lion down against your body to rest until Pierre's parents come home.

As the parents return and deal with the lion, pantomime their parts. Pretend to pull the lion's mane and to hit him over the head with the folding chair. The lion finally answers Mother's question with "I don't care," and Pierre's whereabouts are discovered!

When the doctor shakes the lion up and down, use your other hand on the lion to shake him up and down, with the lion's mouth facing the floor, then pulling your hand back quickly and looking at the children in astonishment as the lion gives a roar. Of course, act surprised as you tell the children Pierre fell out of the lion's mouth!

After Pierre falls out, have the lion settle against you once more until it is time for him to invite Pierre to go for a ride.

After Pierre is shaken out of the lion and is ready to go home, tell the children, "This time Pierre says something different. I'll say it, and then you can say it after me." Say the "I am feeling fine" speech in three sections, pausing at the end of each phrase so the audience can remember the lines and repeat them with you.

Continue narrating the rest of the action, using the lion to show what is happening whenever possible. When it's time for the moral of the story, the lion looks at the audience, says the final word, "care," and then jumps back into his bag.

Completed lion puppet.

Section Two:
Simple Puppet Activities
Children Can Do

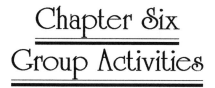

Chapter Six
Group Activities

This chapter and the next describe how to directly involve children in making and using puppets. These activities can all be used as follow-up activities to the scripts in Section 1. Chapter 6 contains activities children do in a group, and all these activities work especially well with preschoolers. Chapter 7 has instructions for children to make simple puppets and use them to tell stories to each other and outside audiences. The activities in Chapter 7 can result in a child telling a story alone, and they work well with primary grade children.

In both chapters the easier scripts are listed first. If the children are new to puppetry, you may want to begin with one of the first lesson plans.

Involving children in telling stories with puppets is a valuable whole language activity. Storytelling builds excitement regarding literature and directly involves children with story structure as well as oral and written language. Storytelling develops imagination and encourages careful listening as well as self-expression.

Adding puppets to the storytelling activity often makes it even more effective. The children become kinesthetically involved in the story by using the puppets to act it out as it is told. Sometimes using a puppet frees a shy child to speak in front of a group. The puppets can also help children remember the sequence of events in the tale they are telling.

Too often, children in groups are taught to make puppets and not taught how to use them. This is a great loss, as there is much to be gained from working with the children in using the puppets.

Plan your program to allow time for using the puppets the children make. Begin with the child-tested, successful activities explained in this section. You will be delighted with the results.

INTRODUCTION

Young children easily and spontaneously bring puppets to life. The activities suggested here will assist you in directing the children's natural playful creativity toward successful puppet activities in groups. These are best suited for preschool through kindergarten children.

WHERE THE WILD THINGS ARE

Story Source: Sendak, Maurice. *Where the Wild Things Are*. New York: Harper & Row, Publishers, 1963.

Characters/Themes: Imagination, Scary Creatures

Ages: 2 to 5

Story Summary: This classic and satisfying story features Max, a young boy sent to bed without his supper because he was acting too wild. Max imagines that he sails away to a land full of wild things and becomes their king. The warm ending shows Max sailing home, where someone loves him best of all.

General Information: In this activity, the children make paper plate "wild thing" puppets and use them to act out the wild rumpus scene in the story.

Audience: Everyone is involved in acting out the story. This activity is not meant to be performed for any audience other than the children involved.

Number of Sessions: one 45-minute session

Materials to Prepare Ahead of Time:

- White paper plates—one and a half per child. The half plate should be stapled to the back of the whole plate before the child decorates the plate. These half plates act as handles for the children to hold as they manipulate their puppets.
- Stapler and staples—to be used by the teacher ahead of time to prepare the paper plates.
- Tissue paper—assorted colors, cut in short strips or small pieces of varied shapes. One fast way to get lots of tissue paper pieces is to buy a tissue paper pom-pom in appropriate wild colors and give it a haircut, cutting the narrow strips into different random lengths, from 1 1/2" to 3" inches long.
- Construction paper pieces—varied colors pre-cut into circles, squares, and triangles to be used for eyes, teeth, or horns. If the children are old enough and there is time, you can allow them to cut out their own shapes.

Other Materials Needed:

- Construction paper—size 9" x 12" for children who wish to draw and cut out bodies for their wild things
- Glue or paste—accessible to each child
- Crayons or water-based felt pens—assorted colors available to each child
- Brads (paper fasteners)—optional, one per child

Lesson Contents

Introduction: Read or tell the story with lots of expression.

Puppet Making: Every child will make a paper plate "wild thing" puppet to act out the wild rumpus scene in the story.

Puppet Head: The round paper plate with the half-plate handle on the back is to be the head of the wild thing. On the plate, the child draws wild thing features, such as scary eyes and an open mouth with lots of teeth. The child can also glue or paste on construction paper shapes for eyes, teeth, horns, or ears.

The tissue paper pieces are the wild thing fur. The child should lightly spread glue or paste everywhere that fur is desired. (Encourage the children not to put glue on the features they have just added to the plate.) Sprinkle lots of tissue paper onto the glue, being sure that parts of the pieces attach with the glue and parts of them stick up to add a furry texture to the face.

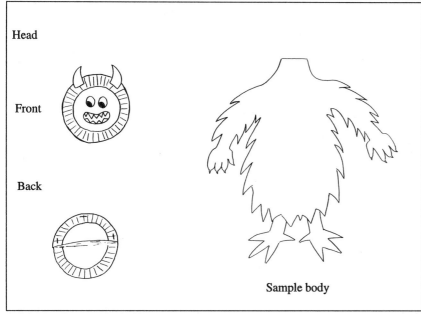

Head

Front

Back

Sample body

Wild thing face and body ideas.

Puppet Body: While the glue is drying, have the child make a body for the wild thing. The body can be drawn, colored, and cut out of construction paper. Be sure the body has a long, thick neck to provide a good strong place to attach it to the head. When the body is complete, it can be stapled to the head or attached with a brad so it can swing below the head during the wild rumpus.

Puppet Performance: Sit on the floor in a circle with the children and their puppets. Use a puppet yourself to demonstrate possible movements the puppets can make during the wild rumpus. Have the children use their puppets to make the movements you are making with your puppet. The children may also suggest other movements to try. The wild things can hop, jump, twist, climb on their owners (but on no one else), roar, gnash their terrible teeth, and roll their eyes by rolling their heads around.

Practice stopping all the puppets in the middle of the wild rumpus when you, playing the part of Max, say "Stop!" and look into their eyes.

At this point, you may let children take turns playing the part of Max and stopping the wild rumpus. Or you may wish to have the children put their puppets face down on the floor in front of them in preparation for the story. You then tell or read the whole story again, with the children picking up their puppets to act out the part when Max comes to the land of the wild things.

THE VERY BUSY SPIDER

Story Source: Carle, Eric. *The Very Busy Spider*. New York: Philomel Books, 1984.

Theme: Ecology

Ages: 2 to 5

Story Summary: Predictable, repetitive dialogue makes this a good choice for puppet performance with young children. Farm animals try to divert a busy little spider from spinning her web. She persists and produces a thing of both beauty and usefulness.

General Information: In this activity, the whole group is involved in acting out the story. Each child makes a spider and one other farm animal stick puppet character. The entire class acts out the story with their puppets while you narrate. The idea for this puppet activity was given to me by Pam Wade of Puppet Pals in Sacramento, California.

Audience: Everyone is involved in acting out the story. This activity is not meant to be performed for any audience other than the children involved.

Number of Sessions: one 45-minute session

Materials to Prepare Ahead of Time:
- White construction paper or tagboard, cut in 2" x 2 1/2" pieces—two per child plus a few extras for children who want to start over or make more puppets.
- If you wish to make patterns for the animals and the fence, these will, of course, need to be prepared ahead of time as well.

Other Materials Needed:
- Popsicle sticks—one per child
- White glue, paste, or tape to attach the puppets to the sticks
- Masking tape to hold the spider puppets on their crayons or felt pens
- Scissors
- Crayons or water-based felt pens in assorted colors for drawing the puppets. Each child will need to use a crayon or felt pen when drawing the web with the spider during the story.
- 8 1/2" x 11" unlined white paper—one per child for the fence and web

Lesson Contents

Introduction: Read or tell the story with lots of expression. If possible, use different voices for the animals as they ask the spider their questions. Encourage the children to join in on the repeated refrain, "The spider didn't answer. She was very busy spinning her web."

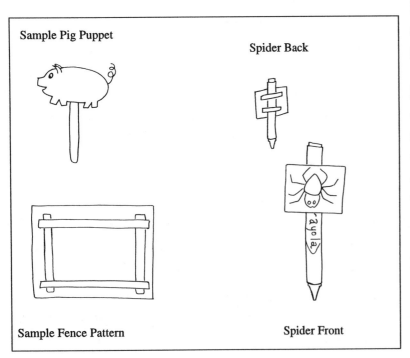

Sample Pig Puppet

Spider Back

Sample Fence Pattern

Spider Front

Puppet Making: Every child will make a spider puppet, one other farm animal puppet, and a fence for the web.

Spiders: To make spider puppets, have the children draw pictures of spiders on their 2" x 2 1/2" pieces of paper. They may cut them out if they wish. Use masking tape to tape each spider to a felt pen or large crayon. Be sure the spider is positioned so that the child can still hold the crayon or pen and draw the web with the spider in place.

Farm Animals: With the children's help, make a list of the farm animals in the story: horse, cow, sheep, goat, pig, dog, cat, duck, rooster, and owl. Make sure that at least one child is making each animal.

If you have more than 10 children in your group, some of the children can make duplicates. Or you and the children can add other farm animals to the story and make up new dialogue for them. For example, a chicken's new dialogue could be "Cluck! Cluck!" called the chicken. "Want to scratch for some corn?"

Each child will draw and color a picture of his or her chosen animal on one of the 2" x 2 1/2" pieces of paper. (You may wish to give the children patterns based on the illustrations in Carle's book.) When the pictures are complete, glue, paste, or tape the animals to popsicle sticks.

Scenery: Have the children draw simple fences on their 8 1/2" x 11" sheets of paper. Demonstrate on the chalkboard what they might wish to draw, based on the illustrations in the book. Or provide them with a ditto of a fence. Whether they draw the fence or you draw it for them, be sure plenty of room is left on the paper for them to draw in webs as they use their spiders to act out the story.

Puppet Performance: Begin by having the children practice walking movements for the farm animal puppets who walk and flying movements for the rooster and the owl. Next practice the sounds the animals make. You can have the whole class make the sounds for each animal as the children make them move. Or have just the individual children manipulating the horses make the sound for the horses, etc. You and the other children can coach the individuals if they cannot think of what to say.

As the narrator begins the story, all the children make their spiders fly through the air to land on their fences and begin to "spin" (draw) their webs.

You will want to change the text of the story slightly so you can cue the children. For example, when it is time for the horse to come on, say: "A horse walked over to the spider and spoke to her." If the children who made horses don't respond, help them with questions like, "What kind of sounds do horses make?" and "What did the horse want the spider to do?" As much as possible, encourage and allow the children to speak for their puppet characters.

Have all the children say the lines about the spider in unison with you as they add another line or two to their webs. As the story ends, the children can make their spiders pounce on the imaginary flies caught in their webs, and finally fall fast asleep.

WHO TOOK THE FARMER'S HAT?

Story Source: Nodset, Joan. *Who Took the Farmer's Hat?* Illustrated by Fritz Siebel. New York: Harper & Row, 1963.

Themes: Ecology, Surprises

Ages: 2 to 6

Story Summary: A farmer loses his round brown hat to the wind. As he asks other creatures if they have seen it, they each describe a round brown "something" that is now gone. Finally, the farmer finds birds in a round brown nest that looks a lot like his old brown hat. He buys himself a new round brown hat.

General Information: This is another story for all the students in the class to perform at once. Each student makes a round brown hat and a two-sided stick puppet with the farmer on one side and another character in the story on the other. This two-sided puppet will pop up out of the round brown hat. The idea for this puppet activity was given to me by Pam Wade of Puppet Pals in Sacramento, California.

Audience: Everyone is involved in acting out the story. This activity is not meant to be performed for any audience other than the children involved.

Number of Sessions: one hour-long session

Materials to Prepare Ahead of Time:
- Small paper cups, the size sometimes found at drinking fountains—one per child with a few extras. Use a sharp bamboo skewer to poke a small hole in the center of the bottom of each cup.
- Either prepare a pattern for the children to trace or just pre-cut out round brown brims from construction paper. These brims are for the hats the children will make. The brims should slide snugly up from the bottom over the small cups and stop under their rims.
- Clip off the sharp ends of enough bamboo skewers for one per child, with a few extras.
- Cut tagboard or white construction paper into 2" x 6" strips—one strip per child plus a few extras.

Other Materials Needed:
- Transparent tape to hold the brims to the paper cup hats.
- Brown crayons or felt pens to color the cups brown on the outside.
- Crayons or pens in assorted colors to draw the puppets.
- Glue or paste accessible to each child to attach the puppet to the stick. You may want to staple the puppets to the sticks so they may be used before the glue dries.

Lesson Contents

Introduction: Read or tell the story to the children. If possible, change your voice for each animal as it replies to the farmer's question. Encourage the children to join in with you on the farmer's repeated lines as you present the story.

Puppet Making: With the children's help, make a list on the chalkboard of all the animal characters in the story. The list should read as follows: squirrel, mouse, fly, goat, duck, and bird. As you list the animals, discuss with the children what each animal thought the hat was. For example, the goat thought it was a flowerpot.

When the list on the board is complete, decide which animal character each child will make. Duplicates are fine, but be sure at least one child is making each animal.

Instructions to give the children:
1. To make the stick puppet, fold the 2" x 6" tagboard in half to create a 2" x 3" shape.
2. Draw and color the farmer on one side, with the fold at the top of your picture.
3. Turn the tagboard over, still keeping the fold at the top. Draw and color a picture of the animal you will be in the story.
4. Put glue or paste on the inside of your pictures and glue them to your bamboo skewer like a peanut butter sandwich. The two pictures are like the slices of bread and the skewer is like the peanut butter inside. You may also staple the pictures to the skewer for extra security.
5. To make the hat, color your cup brown on the outside.
6. Cut out the brim and slide it over the bottom of the cup and up to fit under the rim, as shown in the illustration. Hold the brim in place with three pieces of transparent tape.

Puppet Performance: You tell the beginning of the story as all the children hold the hats on the heads of their stick puppet farmers. As you describe the action, the children pantomime the hats blowing away and the farmers looking all around for their hats.

Then the children slip the farmers' sticks into the hats, so they become pop-up puppets. The children can make the farmer slide out of sight into the hat. Once the farmer is hidden, the puppet can be turned around so the farmer is on the back and the animal shows. The children can choose the proper character and slide it out to speak at the appropriate time. For example, when the farmer meets the squirrel, all the children pop up their farmers and ask his question in unison. Then the children who have made squirrels turn their sticks to show the squirrels and say the squirrel's reply.

If the children do not know what to say, prompt them with questions like "What did the squirrel see up in the sky instead of the farmer's round brown hat?" and "Did the bird have wings?" You could ask the child playing the fly, "What happened to the round brown hill in the tree?" As much as possible, encourage and allow the children to speak for the puppets as they act out the story.

If time allows, do it again. The children love using their puppets to act out the story in this way. The more times they are able to do it, the more comfortable they will be with the story and the more their self-esteem will grow from a fun job well done.

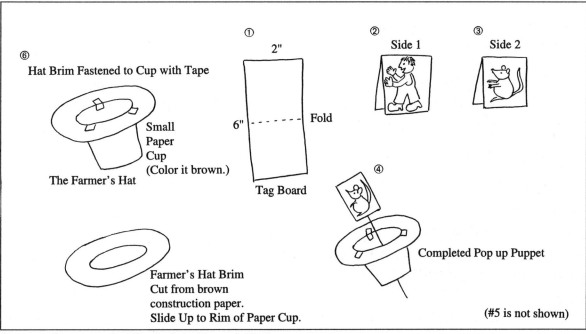

How to make puppets for *Who Took the Farmer's Hat?*

Chapter Seven
Children Telling Stories with Puppets

The activities in this chapter teach the children to tell stories with puppets. In each plan the children learn to tell a story, make the puppet characters needed to act it out, create puppet voices, and perform their work for others. They will manipulate their puppets as their storytelling partners tell the story, or as they tell the story themselves.

If time allows, each child will complete a set of all the puppets and props needed to act out the story so he or she can go home prepared to tell the story to family and friends. Primary grade children are capable of this, and these activities are very effective self-esteem builders. The children are delighted to have their own complete puppet kits to use over and over.

THE TEENY TINY WOMAN
English

Story Source: "The Teeny Tiny Woman" script found in Chapter 5, page 58.

Characters/Themes: Food, Scary Creatures, Surprises

Ages: 4 to 8

General Information: Each student will make a stick puppet and use it to act out the story "The Teeny Tiny Woman." Each child will learn a story, make a simple puppet, manipulate the puppet (using voice to create suspense), and share the work with others.

Audience: Other children in the group

Number of Sessions: one to two sessions of 45 minutes to an hour in length

Materials Needed:
- Popsicle sticks—one per child
- White glue, paste, or tape to attach the puppets to the sticks
- Crayons or water-based felt pens
- Scissors
- White construction paper or other neutral-colored stiff paper such as tagboard or clean file folders—one sheet per child

Overview of Lesson Contents: If only one session is available for this activity, or if the children are ages four and five, do selected activities from the detailed two-session lesson plan that follows. First, tell the story to the children, using a puppet and the script in this book. Then allow them time to make a puppet and quickly rehearse basic puppet movements. Finally, retell the story while the children use their puppets to pantomime the action of the story.

If two sessions are available for this activity, follow the more complete instructions given below.

Session One

What you will accomplish:

- The children will become familiar with the story and see a demonstration of how to use a stick puppet to act out the story as it is told.
- The children will practice saying the line "Give me my bone."
- Each child will construct a teeny tiny woman stick puppet.

How to do it:

1. Tell the story to the children, using the script in this book. To model the puppet action that you will be asking the children to do later, use a finger puppet on a stick or a stick puppet you've made as you tell the story.

   Spend a few minutes with the children on the repeated line, "Give me my bone." Tell them that every time the line is said, it is said a little more loudly. The third and last time the line is said, it is said *very* loudly.

   Have them practice saying that line together while watching your hand signals for volume. If you raise one finger, they will say the line softly. When you hold up two fingers, they will say the line a little more loudly. And when you hold up three fingers, they will say the line as loudly as they can. Work with them on consistently saying the words slowly and deliberately even as they increase the volume each time.

2. After you have presented the story, discuss with the children how they will make their own teeny tiny woman stick puppets. This is a brainstorming session where all ideas are valid. This discussion is to encourage the children to think of many possibilities and to let them know that they are free to make their puppets however they wish.

   To get ideas flowing freely, you may wish to ask some questions: What is your teeny tiny woman wearing? What colors does she like? Does she wear a hat? What do her shoes look like? What color is her hair? Are her arms sticking out or by her sides? Throughout this discussion, remind the children that all ideas are good ones; there are no wrong answers.

3. Give the children the materials they need to make their own teeny tiny woman stick puppets. They will draw the woman on stiff paper, color her, cut her out, and glue, paste, or tape her to a popsicle stick. As much as time allows, let the children make other things they think would add to their story, like a teeny tiny bone prop on a stick or a paper blanket for her to hide under when she hears the voice from the cupboard.

Session Two

What you will accomplish:

- Review of the story with the children, giving them a chance to practice many of the lines in the story.
- The children will use the puppets they made to rehearse the pantomime actions needed to act out the story.
- The children will work with storytelling partners to practice both telling the story and acting it out with their puppets.

How to do it:

1. Begin by reviewing what you did in Session 1 with the repeated line, "Give me my bone." Remind the children that every time the line is said, it is said a little more loudly. The third and last time it is said *very* loudly.

   Briefly have the children practice saying that line together while watching your hand signals for volume. If you raise one finger, they will say the line softly. When you hold up two fingers, they will say the line a little more loudly. And when you hold up three fingers, they will say the line as loudly as they can. Remind them to say the words slowly and deliberately even as they increase the volume each time.

2. Next, tell the story again to the group, using your own teeny tiny woman puppet. Encourage the children to join in as much as possible in your telling. Of course they will all be ready to repeat the line, "Give me my bone," with increased volume each time. Have them all shout "Take it!" as the teeny tiny woman does for the last line of the story.

3. After the children have seen you again tell the story using your puppet, pass out their puppets. All together, discuss and practice the following pantomimes:

   Walking—move the puppet up and down as well as forward. The puppet should look in the direction it is going whenever possible and remain a consistent height in relation to the ground.

   Showing surprise—at seeing the teeny tiny bone lying on the ground have the teeny tiny woman take a small jump back and make some sound like a "gasp!" or whatever sound each storyteller feels is appropriate.

   Picking up the teeny tiny bone—bend down over your other hand outstretched at imaginary ground level and stand back up. Because a stick puppet like this cannot really pick anything up, extra imagination is required here. It also helps a great deal if either the storyteller or the teeny tiny woman herself says what she is doing. So have the children practice saying "As she picked up the teeny tiny bone she said, 'Oh, won't this teeny tiny bone make a wonderful teeny tiny soup for my teeny tiny supper,'" as they pantomime picking up the bone.

   Going to sleep—have the teeny tiny woman hide her eyes by turning her back to the audience. The children can practice having their puppets climb imaginary stairs and go to sleep on their shoulders, using their free hands as blankets for their puppets to snuggle and hide under. When the teeny tiny woman hides her eyes, the audience can imagine that they are closed because she is sleeping.

   Showing fear—as she hears the voice speaking to her from the teeny tiny cupboard have the teeny tiny woman tremble slightly. Each time the voice gets louder the teeny tiny woman will tremble more violently.

110

4. After the children have practiced these movements thoroughly, narrate the story as the whole group pantomimes the action and joins in on the repeated refrains. Then, begin retelling the story with the children pantomiming the action with their puppets. During this second telling, ask for volunteers to tell segments of the story so they get experience telling the story themselves. This is the final rehearsal before you divide them into pairs for storytelling practice.

5. Next, assign each child a storytelling partner. One child tells the story while the other acts it out with the puppet. When the story is finished, they trade roles so that the storyteller becomes the puppeteer for the next telling. As the children are working in pairs, circulate among them, listening and giving advice and encouragement. Also watch for teams who are doing well enough to be sent to perform for other groups of children.

At the end of the session, encourage the children to take their puppets home and retell the story to their family and friends.

WIDE-MOUTHED FROG
Traditional

Story Source: "Wide-Mouthed Frog" script found in Chapter 5, page 60.

Characters/Themes: Ecology, Humor, Jungle Beasts, Food

Ages: 6 to 8

Story Summary: A wide-mouthed frog is so proud of her new babies that she feels they are too good to eat flies like regular frogs. She goes off in search of more appropriate food, asking other mothers what they feed their babies. She's quite startled to find that Ms. Crocodile feeds her babies wide-mouthed frogs!

General Information: In this activity, each child makes a wide-mouthed frog puppet with a moving mouth, using folded green construction paper. The children use these frogs to act out the story as you have modeled it for them. If you have enough time to rehearse, each child can learn the story well enough to tell it using a puppet.

Audience: The first time, there is no audience. Everyone acts out the story by using their puppets to say the frog's lines as you narrate the rest. If time permits, the children can all learn the story, so that each child can tell it using a puppet. Then they may perform for small groups of their peers, their families, or they may take the story to share with another class or a few people in a nursing home.

Number of Sessions: One session, one hour in length, is all that is needed to make the frogs and perform the story as a group. Another session should be added if you wish each child to learn the story well enough to perform it alone, using a puppet.

Materials to Prepare Ahead of Time:

- Green construction paper, 9" x 12"—two sheets per child, one for the head and one for the body. If the children are young, you may wish to lightly prefold into thirds the sheet that will be used for the head, as folding it into thirds is the most difficult part. You may also wish to give young children a simple pattern for the body that they will cut out. Older children can draw their own bodies.

Wide Mouthed Frog—ready to tell her story!

Other Materials Needed:

- Scissors
- Crayons to draw the frog features and bodies
- Transparent tape or staples and stapler to attach the head once it is folded and to attach the frog bodies to their heads.

Session One

Introduction: Tell the story using a frog puppet, modeling the puppet action the children will be doing when they use their newly made frog puppets to tell the story again.

Puppet Making: Every child will make a wide-mouthed frog puppet from folded paper.

Puppet Head: Crease each fold well in the following steps that are described and pictured here:

1. Fold one piece of 9" x 12" green construction paper lengthwise into thirds.

2. Fold in half, making your paper into a "V" shape with the loose flap on the outside of the "V."

3. Fold one side of the "V" in half by bringing it back to meet the center fold, making your paper into an "H" shape.

4. Turn the paper over and repeat step 3, making your paper a "W" or "M" shape.

5. Now you have created a pocket for your fingers and a pocket for your thumb, as illustrated on the next page. Tape or staple these pockets together, leaving just one thickness of construction paper to rise above the fingers and one thickness to curve below the thumb. This makes it easier for children to find the pockets for their fingers and thumb.

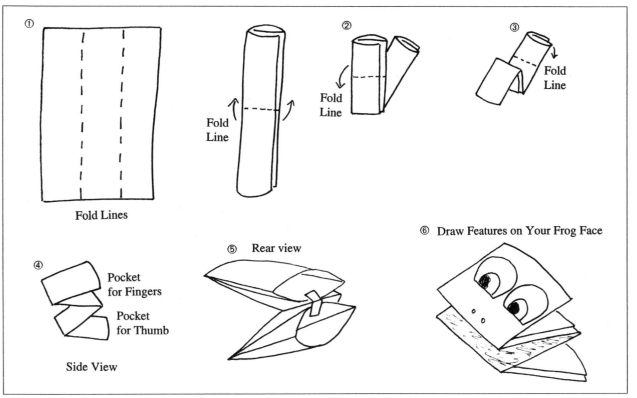

① Fold Lines

② Fold Line Fold Line

③ Fold Line

④ Pocket for Fingers Pocket for Thumb Side View

⑤ Rear view

⑥ Draw Features on Your Frog Face

Wide-Mouthed Frog

6. Draw frog eyes, warts, and any other decorations you wish on your frog. Perhaps you'd like to give her a tongue on the inside of her mouth.

Puppet Body: Have the children design and cut out frog bodies or cut out frog body patterns you provide. A sample frog body pattern is included on the next page. Notice the extra paper at the neck. This is to be folded forward on the dotted line and stapled or taped to the bottom jaw of the frog's head.

Puppet Performance: First, have all the children use their puppets to practice lip syncing (moving the mouths as if they are talking) with you. Remind them that for most of the story they will want to open their frogs' mouths as wide as they can without tearing the paper. Also practice opening the frogs' mouths just a little to say the final lines. If you need more information on lip syncing, refer to Chapter 8.

With the children's help, make a list on the chalkboard of all the mothers Ms. Frog meets, in the order she will meet them. The list should read turtle, deer, owl, and crocodile. This will help the children know what is coming next as they participate in the retelling of the story.

Discuss what foods the mothers recommended and why Ms. Frog rejected them. Practice all together using the puppets to open their mouths very wide and say, "What do you feed your babies?" and to say Ms. Frog's response to each mother's reply.

Tell the story again, using your puppet and having the children all use their puppets to say as many of Ms. Frog's lines as they can remember.

If this is all the time you have, encourage the children to take their puppets home and tell the story again to their family and friends. Let the children know that when they tell the story on their own, they can add other animal mothers for Ms. Frog to visit and make up appropriate lines for them to say.

Session Two

If you have time for another session, keep the frogs at school and spend the second session on storytelling. Some suggestions follow for assisting the students in learning the story so well they can tell it on their own. Additional ideas for practicing appear in other story plans in this chapter.

1. Begin session 2 by using your frog puppet to tell the story again yourself. Encourage the children to join in on the lines they already know.

2. Right after you finish telling the story, have each child draw a comic strip of the story, showing each scene. The children can use the completed comic strips as prompts if they need a reminder of what comes next as they tell the story to each other.

3. Divide the class into teams of two. One tells the story while the partner listens; then they switch. If the storyteller gets stuck, the listener can help out by asking appropriate questions or giving hints about what comes next. They can use their comic strips as a guide. Circulate among them to help and to choose the most successful tellers. You may want to ask one or two children to tell their versions in front of the whole class, for additional modeling.

THE GUNNY WOLF
African-American

Story Source: "The Gunny Wolf" script found in Chapter 5, page 69.

Characters/Themes: Scary Creatures, Wolves

Ages: 6 to 8

Goals: Each student will make a puppet kit consisting of stick puppet characters and scenery necessary to tell the story of "The Gunny Wolf." The children will learn to tell the story and practice telling it, using the puppet kits they make. Each child will have the opportunity to perform the story with puppets for at least one other child.

Audience: Their peers, another class, a preschool group, a nursing home, or a parent group

Number of Sessions: two to four sessions of 45 minutes to an hour in length

Materials Needed:
- Popsicle sticks—three per child
- White glue, paste, or tape to attach the puppets to the sticks
- Crayons or water-based felt pens
- Scissors
- White construction paper or other neutral-colored stiff paper—two to three sheets per child

Overview of Lesson Contents:
Session One: Read or tell the story to the students. Discuss the puppets and scenery they will be making, and allow the children to begin construction.

Session Two: Begin by going over the story again with the children. Spend the rest of the time completing the construction of the puppets and scenery. If this is the final session, have the children perform for each other in pairs, manipulating the puppets as you tell the story. All the children will join in saying the repeated lines they know.

Session Three: Dedicate the session to rehearsal and performance.

Session Four: Have the children perform their puppet plays for another class, a preschool group, a nursing home, a parent group, or another receptive audience.

Session One: Introduction

1. Tell the story to the children, using the script found in this book. If possible use puppets to tell them the story, as using puppets will model for them the puppet action they will be doing later. Invite the children to join you in singing the song the little girl sings as she goes into the forest to pick the flowers. Also encourage the children to join you in saying the repeated refrains in the story, so that the children are already learning the lines and voices they will be using to tell the story with puppets.

Refrains they will want to repeat with you include:

Gunny wolf: Little girl, why for you move?

Little girl: Oh, I no move.

Gunny wolf: Then you sing that goodest, sweetest song again, all right?

The children can also join in on the sound effects of the chase scene, when the little girl goes "pit pat, pit pat" and the Gunny Wolf goes "hunker che, hunker che, hunker che."

2. After you have presented the story, discuss with the children what puppet characters and scenery they will need to act it out. This is a brainstorming session where all ideas are valid. This discussion is to encourage the children to think of many possibilities and to let them know that they are free to make their puppets and scenery however they wish.

The puppet list will include little girl, Gunny Wolf, and mother. Following are some sample questions you might ask to encourage brainstorming: Does anyone *really* know what a gunny wolf looks like? Will your gunny wolf have a tail? What size will you make the gunny wolf's ears? eyes? paws? Will the gunny wolf be bigger than the little girl? How will the mother be dressed? What color will you make the little girl's hair?

Then discuss the necessary scenery. After you've agreed that each play will need a forest and the little girl's house and yard, ask the children some questions about how they will draw them. Throughout this discussion, remind the children that everyone's ideas are valid.

Ask the children: How will the forest look? Where should the flowers be in the forest? (Remind them they will need three areas with flowers, to lure the little girl deeper and deeper into the forest.) What color will your flowers be? (They do not have to be the same colors that you said in your story, so each child may choose three colors to make the flowers in his or her play.) What will you make the little girl's house look like? Will she have any trees in her yard? Will she have toys in her yard?

3. After the discussion, show the children the materials you have for them to make the puppets and scenery. Have them use one 9" x 12" sheet of white construction paper to draw and color the puppets. As they finish their drawings, they cut out the pictures and glue, paste, or tape each character to a popsicle stick. While the glue is drying, begin working on the scenery.

For the scenery, have each child fold a single sheet of construction paper in half, drawing the forest on one side and the house and yard on the other. Staple or tape the paper together at the bottom. Yarn is tied to the top of the scenery on both sides so the scenery can be worn around the storyteller's neck. The storyteller can stand in front of a small audience and look down at the scenery as he or she moves the puppets in front of the scenery. It will be necessary to experiment with the length of the yarn so the scenery hangs at a comfortable height for the puppeteer to manipulate the puppets in front of it and so that it can easily be turned over twice during the story. When the little girl enters the forest, the scenery is turned over to show the forest, and the scenery is turned again to show the house as the little girl runs "pit pat, pit pat" home to be "goodest, sweetest safe."

Usually some children will have different ideas for scenery construction. It is nice to allow as much freedom as time permits. One child may want to make the scenery stand up like a tent on the desk and to stand beside it to move the puppets and tell the story. Another child may want a slit in a bush so the gunny wolf can pop up and scare the little girl. Someone else's house scenery may get so complicated with doors that open and cutout windows for the little girl to see out that a second piece of paper may be needed for the forest.

The ideas the children have are often much more advanced than my original plan, and even more delightful! I love to allow them to take a project and fly with their own creativity and imagination. Try to have a schedule flexible enough to accommodate these ideas whenever possible.

The final step is to construct a folder for each individual puppet kit, so the kits can be transported safely home after performances for the group. A large piece of construction paper, folded in half and glued or taped shut along the sides, will work. Leave the top open for puppets and scenery to be put in.

Session Two: Construction of Puppets and Scenery

1. Begin the session by telling the story again, encouraging even more participation from the children. As you tell the story this time, try calling on individual children to speak particular lines in the story. Pause occasionally to let volunteers help you fill in the next story segment. In this way, you encourage the children to know that they, too, can tell the story.

2. For the remainder of the session, the children work on completing their puppets and scenery. Circulate among them, answering questions and talking with them about how they will use their puppets and scenery to tell the story.

Session Three: Rehearsal

1. Begin this session by working with the children on puppet manipulation. Each child will use completed puppets to practice the movements necessary to tell the story. Ask for their suggestions and demonstrations, add your own, and have the whole group practice with their puppets at the same time. The basic movements that you want to include are as follows:

Walking—move the puppet up and down as well as forward. The puppet should look in the direction it is going whenever possible.

Running—move in a more exaggerated walk, leaning forward and moving faster.

Picking flowers—bend down over the flower bed and stand back up. Because a stick puppet like this cannot really pick anything up, extra imagination is required here. It also helps a great deal if either the storyteller or the little girl herself says what she is doing. So have the children practice saying "And she picked the white flower" as they pantomime picking a flower.

Showing surprise—jump back as the gunny wolf appears, accompanied by a "gasp!" or whatever sound each storyteller feels is appropriate.

Showing fear—as the gunny wolf talks to the little girl have her tremble slightly.

Going to sleep—the gunny wolf somehow hides his eyes as he reclines and possibly snores as the little girl is singing to him. When he hides his eyes, the audience can imagine that they are closed because he is sleeping.

2. After the children have practiced these movements thoroughly, narrate the story as the whole group pantomimes the action and joins in on the songs, repeated refrains, and sound effects. This is the final rehearsal before you break them into groups for individuals to have turns telling the story with their puppet kits.

3. Depending on the time remaining in the session, assign the children to storytelling groups of two or three. In the groups, each child takes a turn telling the story and acting it out with the puppets while the other group members act as an audience. If you think the children are not quite ready to handle the parts of both the storyteller and the puppeteer at one time, instruct one child to tell the story while the other acts out the story with puppets. Then they will switch roles, so that each child has the experience of being the storyteller as well as the puppeteer.

A child rehearses with his puppet kit of "The Gunny Wolf."

Session Four: Performance

1. If time permits a fourth session, the children will be able to perform their story for another class or for other people. You may set up these performances in several ways, depending on what audiences can be arranged and what you feel the children can comfortably do.

The simplest performance consists of you narrating the story while a group of children stand in front of the audience and act out the story with their own puppets and scenery. Another way to arrange a performance is to send a performance team to each audience. One member of the team tells the story; the other member is the puppeteer. This way the children do not have so much to remember, which could be stressful, and they can pick the part they do best—storytelling or puppetry—to perform.

No matter how the performances were planned, begin this performance session with a rehearsal before taking the children to perform before an unfamiliar group.

THE THREE BILLY GOATS GRUFF
Norwegian

Story Source: "The Three Billy Goats Gruff" script found in Chapter 5, page 77.

Characters/Themes: Families, Food, Scary Creatures

Ages: 5 to 8

General Information:
1. Each student will make a puppet kit consisting of stick puppet characters and scenery necessary to tell "The Three Billy Goats Gruff."
2. The children will learn to tell the story and practice telling it using the puppet kits they make.
3. Each child will have the opportunity to perform the story with puppets for at least one other child.

Audience: Their classmates, another class, a preschool group, a nursing home, or a parent group

Number of Sessions: three to four sessions of 45 minutes to an hour in length

Materials Needed:
- Popsicle sticks—four per child
- White glue or paste to attach the puppets to the sticks
- Crayons or water-based felt pens
- Scissors
- White construction paper or other neutral-colored stiff paper—two to three sheets per child

Overview of Lesson Contents

Session One: Read or tell the story to the students. Discuss the puppets and scenery they will be making, and allow the children to begin construction.

Session Two: Begin by going over the story again with the children. The rest of the time will be spent completing the construction of the puppets and scenery.

Session Three: Dedicate session to rehearsal and performance.

Session Four: Have the children perform their puppet plays for another class, a preschool group, a nursing home, or a parent group.

Instructions: A minimum of three sessions are necessary for the children to become familiar with the story, make the puppets, practice puppet movement and voices, and perform the play. By following these directions, each child will have a complete set of puppets to take home and perform for parents, siblings, and friends.

If only two sessions are available for this activity, eliminate the time needed for the children to make the puppets, and do the remainder of the activities listed here with a set of puppets you provide. Choose volunteers to take turns manipulating the puppets you provide. Switch puppeteers often so that many children will have the opportunity to work with the puppets. You will want to have each puppet character handled by a different child each time the story is told, so that more children will be involved. Also, choose a different child as storyteller for each scene to give more opportunity for participation. This will provide an opportunity for the children to experience puppet manipulation, voice, and performance without actually making the puppets.

If one session is all that is available, the children will still get an idea of what is involved. However, only one or two selected groups of children will actually experience performing with the puppets you provide. With this introduction, some children will make puppet kits at home and complete the experience themselves.

Session One

1. Read or tell the children "The Three Billy Goats Gruff." The best introduction would be for you to tell the children the story with puppets, based on the script found in this book, modeling puppet voices and action for them.

As you present the story, invite the children to join in on the repeated refrains, so that they are already beginning to learn the lines and voices they will be using to tell the story with puppets. The following are samples of the type of lines they can begin to say with you right away:

Troll: Who's that tripping over my bridge?

Goat: (Voice pitch will depend on the size of the goat. The amount of fear in the voice will also depend on which goat is speaking.) It is I, the (first, second, or third) Billy Goat Gruff. I'm going up to the hillside to eat grass and get fat.

Troll: Oh no you're not. I'm coming to gobble you up!

2. After you have presented the story, discuss with the children what puppet characters and scenery they will need to act it out. The puppet list will include the troll and the three goats—one little, one middle-sized, and one big. Necessary scenery includes a dry, barren land; an enticing hillside; and a bridge over a river. The bridge must lead from the bare land to the green hillside.

This is a brainstorming session where all ideas are valid. This discussion is to encourage the children to think of many possibilities and to let them know that they are free to make their puppets and scenery however they wish.

To encourage discussion and imaginative thinking, you may want to ask questions similar to the following: What does the troll look like? How tall is it? Is it hairy all over? What color is it? How could you make the three goats look different from one another? Will they all have beards, horns, etc.? What could you put on the hillside that would make the goats want to go there badly enough that they would cross the bridge and risk an encounter with the troll? Throughout the discussion, keep reminding the children that there are no right answers and that all ideas are valid.

3. After the discussion, show the children the materials you have for them to make the puppets and scenery. Have them use one 9" x 12" sheet of white construction paper to draw and color the puppets.

Remind them before they begin to draw the puppets that all the goats must face the same direction and the troll must face the opposite direction. This is important because as the goats cross the bridge they all need to go from the barren side to the enticing hillside, so they all need to face the same direction. As they cross the bridge, the troll jumps up and needs to be facing the goats so they can talk with each other.

When the drawings of the puppet characters are finished, the children cut them out and glue or paste each one onto a popsicle stick. While the glue is drying, have the children begin working on their scenery. In this instance, all three parts of the scene—barren field, bridge, and grassy hillside—need to be included in one picture.

The scenery will be strung on yarn to hang around the storyteller's neck as the story is told and the puppets moved against the scenery. This allows the storyteller to stand in front of a group and tell the story with puppets. Be open to variations that the children think of in making their individual scenery.

The final step is to construct a folder for each individual puppet kit, so the puppets and scenery can be transported safely home after performances. A large sheet of construction paper folded in half and glued or taped up the sides makes a good folder. The top is left open so the puppets and scenery can be put inside.

Session Two

1. Begin the session by telling the story again, encouraging even more participation from the children. This time, as you tell the story, you may call on individual children to say particular lines in the story. Pause occasionally to let volunteers help you fill in the next story segment. Everyone joins in on the sound effects as the goats cross the bridge. In this way you show the children that they, too, can tell the story.

2. For the remainder of the session the children work on completing their puppets and scenery. Circulate among them, answering questions and talking with them about how they will use their puppets and scenery to tell the story.

Session Three

1. Begin this session by working with the children on puppet manipulation. Each child will use completed puppets to practice the movements necessary to tell the story. Ask for their suggestions and demonstrations, add your own, and use your puppets to practice with the children. You need to include the following basic movements:

Walking—move the puppet up and down as well as forward. The puppet should look in the direction it is going whenever possible and maintain a consistent height in relation to the ground.

Running—move the puppets in a more exaggerated walk, leaning forward and moving faster.

Eating grass and flowers—bend down over the grass and flowers and make contented chewing and chomping sounds before standing back up.

Showing surprise—have the goats jump back as the troll appears from under the bridge, accompanied by a bleat! or whatever sound each storyteller feels is appropriate.

Showing fear—as the troll threatens to eat the goat, show the goat trembling slightly as he listens to the troll and replies to his threats.

Fighting—talk with the children about how fights are simulated on television. The fighters never really touch each other. When one punches forward, the other falls backward as if from the blow. Sometimes they move quickly, sometimes more slowly, and sometimes they stop to rest a moment. This discussion is necessary, or sometimes the first rehearsal of the fight between the troll and the biggest goat results in puppets damaged from direct hits.

2. After the children have practiced these movements thoroughly, narrate the story as the whole group pantomimes the actions and joins in on the repeated refrains and sound effects. This is the final rehearsal before they break into groups for individuals to have turns telling the story with their puppet kits.

3. Depending on the time remaining in the session, have the children break into groups of two or three. In the groups, each child takes a turn telling the story with the puppets while the other group members act as an audience. If you think the children are not quite ready to handle the parts of both the storyteller and the puppeteer, instruct one child to tell the story while the other acts out the story with puppets. Then they will switch roles, so that each child has the experience of being the storyteller as well as the puppeteer.

Session Four

1. If time permits a fourth session, the children will be able to perform their plays for another class or for other people. You may set up these performances in several ways, depending on what audiences can be arranged and what you feel the children can comfortably do.

The simplest performance consists of you narrating the story while a group of children stand in front of the audience and act out the story with their own puppets and scenery. Another way is to send a performance team to each audience. One member of the team tells the story; the other member is the puppeteer. This way the children do not have so much to remember, which could be stressful, and they can pick the part they do best to perform.

No matter how the performances are planned, begin the fourth session with a rehearsal before taking the children to perform before an unfamiliar group.

Section Three:
Puppetry Hints and
Resources

Chapter 8
Beyond the Basics

Ten Common Problems and Easy Solutions

It is not necessary to read this section before beginning your work with puppets. You may wish to refer to it if you have questions or problems as you use the scripts in this book. You may also wish to read it as time allows to enhance your knowledge of the power and possibilities puppets can bring to work with young children.

1. Puppet Voices

I don't have a voice for my puppet, and I don't want one!

It is not necessary for your puppet to speak out loud. Refer to the puppet action detailed in the "Peanut Butter/Jelly!" song for one way that a silent puppet can still communicate by whispering in the puppeteer's ear. The puppeteer can then tell the children what the puppet has just said. Another solution is to use one of the commercial puppets with a squeaker inside. The puppet can squeak, and you can tell the children what it is saying.

Sometimes, children will try to insist that the puppet speak for itself rather than whisper to you. Always have the puppet handle these requests. The best solution is for the puppet to demonstrate that it is just too shy to talk. The children seem to accept this. After all, the more they insist that the puppet speak, the more shy and scared it becomes. The children see that they must be gentle, or the puppet will disappear from view and refuse to return.

How can I develop a voice for my puppet?

If you do feel ready to develop a voice for your puppet, remember this saying: "A puppet's character is the key to its voice." In other words, a bossy lion is bound to have a different voice than a timid pig. A sassy baby bear

If you do not choose to create a distinct voice for your puppet, you may want to have it communicate by whispering in your ear.

will definitely sound quite unlike a long-suffering mama bear.

Play with your voice to discover what it can do. As you use your voice in new ways, always be aware of how your voice is feeling. If you feel any strain or feel the need to cough, stop immediately and eliminate that sound from your repertoire.

Start simply by speaking at a higher or lower pitch than you normally do. Then try adding a nasal quality. Experiment with the speed as well as the pitch and tone of your voice. A turtle and a rabbit might partially indicate their characters simply by the speed at which they speak and move.

Pay attention to the voices around you. Try imitating them. Imitate your friends, your family, famous people, and cartoon characters. The key to puppet voice discovery and development is to have fun and to let yourself go. The next section will address how to keep the voice you discover for your puppet.

To summarize the search for a puppet voice, remember these points:

1. A puppet's character is the key to its voice.
2. Play with your voice to see what it can do.
3. Try altering the pitch (higher or lower), the tone (nasal, haughty, blustering, etc.), and the speed (faster or slower).
4. Listen attentively and imitate voices you hear to expand your range and your repertoire.

When I am using my puppet, I get its voice mixed up with my voice.

Once you have discovered a voice that you feel is right for a particular puppet character, the challenge is to remember the voice and re-create it each time the character speaks.

If you have a tape recorder, recording the voice can be very helpful in the beginning. With the voice on tape, you can refer to it each time you begin a new practice session with the puppet. Thus you will avoid the distressing experience of discovering the perfect voice for your puppet one day and not being able to remember that voice the next time you need it.

In addition to using a tape recorder to help you remember the voice at first, the other main tip on keeping the voices straight is to create an "anchor" for the voice within each puppet's character. This anchor could be a laugh, a song, an absent-minded muttering, or an emphatic word the character says a lot. Often the anchor can add interest to the puppet character, and you will want to use it every time the puppet enters. Other times, you will want to move from always voicing the anchor aloud to simply hearing it in your head to remind you of how the character's voice sounds as you begin to speak for the character.

Try laughing a witchy cackle and then following the laugh with some dialogue in a witch's voice. For most of us, it is much easier to sound like a witch after creating that laugh. Your witch character could always begin to speak with a quick, evil cackle. Eventually you will begin to hear the cackle in your mind and be able to go right into the witch voice without laughing aloud first.

Another character may always enter singing the same wordless tune, like "do di o do . . . di o do." For some people songs are easier to remember than words, so it is easier for the puppeteer to make the puppet's sound while singing. If the puppet always enters singing, the puppeteer easily gets into the voice for that character. Just like the witch laugh, eventually you will be able to hear the tune in your head and use it to go into the voice of the character without first singing the tune aloud.

Once I had a ghost character who was famous for his very loud, drawn-out, emphatic stating of the word *Nooooooo*. I could hear in my head how the ghost said that word, and that would help me to remember and use his voice whenever he spoke.

Now that I have a voice for my puppet, how do I make it look like it is really talking or singing?

If your puppet has a moving mouth, use a mirror to work on making appropriate mouth movements. Use the puppet's mouth only for talking and for showing feelings. Many beginning puppeteers flap the puppet's mouth open and shut as it walks, and their puppet looks ridiculous rather than looking alive. Remember, puppets walk with their feet, not with their mouths. Use the mouth movements deliberately to create the illusion of life.

Now you are ready to work on lip sync, the art of moving your puppet's mouth in time with its words to create the illusion that it is really talking. When your puppet is talking, think of pushing the words out from the back of the puppet's throat, rather than biting them. Also, concentrate on moving your thumb up and down to move the jaw, rather than lifting your fingers and the top of the puppet's jaw up, as it speaks. These tips create the most realistic mouth movement. Be sure to always open your puppet's mouth when it starts to talk and close it when it is finished. Don't let your puppet stand around with its mouth half open, unless that would show us something about its character.

Do not try to move your puppet's mouth on every syllable, unless the puppet is speaking ver-y de-lib-er-ate-ly. Instead, move the mouth at a comfortable speed that reflects the speed at which the puppet is talking. When singing with the puppet, be sure to hold the mouth open on any extended notes, such as "mountaaainnn" in "The Bear Went Over the Mountain."

If your puppet does not have a mouth that moves, it is your job to discover what the puppet *can* move to create the illusion that it is talking or singing. If it is singing, perhaps it can move its head or clap its paws in time with the music. If it is talking, it can act out what it is saying through gestures and body language. The scripts contain extensive notes to assist you with this.

A child in the audience shouts, "Your lips are moving!"

Occasionally a child will say, "Your lips are moving!" as I am doing the voice for a puppet I'm using. I have the puppet respond to that comment with utter astonishment. The puppet will turn to me and watch my lips move while it says, "Wow, isn't that amazing. When I talk, her lips move." Then the puppet will turn to look at the audience and comment, "Look at that! I can make her lips move any time I want, just by talking."

The humor with which the puppet responds usually diffuses the situation entirely and even assists in creating the illusion that the puppet is a separate being with a mind of its own. If you always have your puppet respond as if it does have a brain and a unique personality, the illusion of the puppet's life will be easy to maintain.

2. Puppet Movement

My puppets all move the same way. It's boring.

The focus of this book is on puppet action, with the knowledge that puppet movement is one of the most important tools in creating the illusion of life. Therefore, if you have more than one puppet character, you will want to create unique movements for each one.

Just as the puppet's character is the key to its voice, so character is also the key to its movement. Movement is affected by the characteristics of age, size, and attitude. Imagine how an old, wise elephant would move differently from a young, cocky mouse. Think of Aesop's fable about the tortoise and the hare and consider how the animals demonstrated their character through movement. The young, boastful hare moved quickly but inconsistently, while the rock-steady tortoise moved with painful slowness and with a steadfastness that won the race.

Once you have developed a movement style for a particular puppet, it is wise to "anchor" that movement in the same way you anchor the voice. Use the puppet's rate of speech, a song that it sings, a sound that means that character to you, or a visualization of that character moving through life with its own style. With one of these anchors for each puppet, you will be able to give each character its own unique way of moving.

Perhaps your tortoise speaks with the same painstaking slowness that it moves. The lively song that the little red hen sings to get into her voice may also reflect the joyful way that she moves in the world. A sound you hear in your head of "swisssh, swisssh, swisssh" could remind you of how the bear sways back and forth as he walks.

3. "I Can See Your Hand"

A child in the audience shouts, "I can see your hand is inside there!"

At a certain developmental stage, young children are working very hard to distinguish fantasy from reality. They may feel resentful if they think you are trying to trick them by acting like the puppet is alive when it is not. Yet they also are delighted by the puppet creature that you are sharing with them and suspect that it is alive even though they can see that your hand is inside it.

Whenever you detect this conflict in the children be quick to reassure them that their perception is correct. You might respond with a statement like "Yes, my hand is inside because this is a puppet, and we are pretending that this puppet is alive. Let's make believe that it is a real monster (or bunny or goat or whatever the puppet is), and then it can help us with this story (or song or activity)."

This response is very satisfying to the children and yet it does not destroy the fun for the audience. They all know what it means to pretend, and the response gives them permission to throw themselves wholeheartedly into the play without worrying about being tricked.

4. Precocious Children

Sometimes kids say I'm singing the song, or telling the story, wrong.

This is a pretty easy one to handle, if you just keep your self-confidence. If you suspect that this may happen because you are presenting a story the children have probably heard before, introduce the story by saying that the version you are telling is the way you learned the story. Suggest that as they listen, they think about the ways that the story they know is different from the story as you are telling it. After the story, be careful to allow at least a small amount of time to discuss the differences in the story or song versions.

This discussion can be quite valuable, pointing out that often there is no one right way to do something, but rather many different possibilities.

5. Frightened or Shy Preschoolers

My preschoolers are afraid of my puppet.

Just as many preschoolers are afraid of clowns, they are also afraid of puppets. Remember that the world is very new to preschoolers. Everything is real to them, which can be an advantage with puppetry because preschoolers are very willing to believe in the puppets. This developmental phase, however, requires a high degree of sensitivity on the part of the puppeteer. Imagine how you would feel if a big furry monster suddenly jumped onto your lap!

It's the puppeteer's responsibility to create puppet characters that will enchant rather than frighten the open mind and heart of the preschool child. This is not difficult to do once you are aware of the possibility that the child may be frightened of the puppet. Even a puppet monster can become a trusted friend if it is manipulated appropriately. Guidelines for successful puppetry with preschoolers follow:

a. When you introduce a new puppet to preschoolers, move the puppet slowly. Avoid fast, jerky, or unpredictable movements with the puppet.

b. A new puppet character should move quietly at first, without shouting or making loud noises.

c. Keep the puppet well away from the children when they first see it, and only move it closer as they become more comfortable with it and are willing for it to be closer.

d. Offer the children a safe way to interact with the puppet. One thing that often works, even with a monster puppet, is to have the puppet taste fingers. Demonstrate by offering the puppet your finger, which he gently nibbles. Then he whispers in your ear what you taste like, and you tell the children. Have your puppet promise to be very gentle as he tastes fingers. Then say that all people who want to have their fingers tasted should stay sitting down and hold their fingers out in front of them. Your puppet can go around the circle of children and gently nibble each outstretched finger, whispering to you what each child tastes like. Tell each child what the puppet whispers to you. Most children find this great fun.

Never insist that a reluctant child have his or her finger tasted. If a reluctant child is sitting on a parent's lap, have the puppet offer to taste the parent's finger. The puppet is always extra gentle when tasting a parent's finger. Often this example gives the child the courage to offer his or her finger to the puppet. If the child is not with a parent or older sibling, then I will ask if the child wants to shake the puppet's hand or pat its head instead. I may show the children how much the puppet likes to be stroked. Sometimes they will want to do this. Always move slowly and give the children total authority in how far they want to go in interacting with the puppet.

e. If you are working with a child who appears shy or frightened, it helps to have the puppet mirror the child's feelings by acting shy or frightened. Point out to the child that the puppet is feeling those feelings, too, and offer some suggestions of what the child could do to make the puppet feel better.

If the child is too frightened or too shy to actually touch the puppet, the puppeteer could encourage the child to just smile at the puppet. When the child smiles, the puppeteer then coaxes the puppet to look at the child and see the smile. The puppet could be willing to quit hiding its face and quietly turn to look at the child. This is the beginning of trust between the child and the puppet. As the child begins to feel more comfortable, the child could be encouraged to gently pat or stroke the puppet, who is still acting shy. This would cause the puppet to very slowly turn its face toward the child and make some gentle gesture of contentment. The puppet could sigh deeply, nod its head, snuggle down contentedly, or present another part of its body for petting as well.

f. Always let the children be in control of their direct interactions with the puppet.

Keep the puppet gentle and quiet as long as the children are hesitant. Friendships between the children and the puppet are sure to follow this sensitive beginning. After the friendship is established, the puppet may become more rambunctious if its character calls for it.

6. Controlling the Audience

When I am trying to lead an activity with a puppet, some children crowd around, insisting on touching and holding the puppet. The focus is on the puppet, not the activity, and I feel out of control.

Let the puppet respond and help you regain control in this situation. How the puppet responds will depend on its character.

A puppet who is shy anyway will be overwhelmed by the children's demands. If children get too close, the puppet will instantly hide. You can explain to the children that the puppet is not comfortable unless the children are sitting in their places. Wait for them all to be settled into their places once more before the puppet peeks out to see if it is safe to come back out.

A puppet who is boastful, or an earnest puppet who is simply trying to make a point, will be frustrated that it cannot be heard if the children are standing up and trying to touch it. The puppet will stomp off and disappear into its bag. Explain to the children that your puppet feels very frustrated if people do not listen, and that it will return only when everyone is ready to listen. Then wait for everyone to be settled before the puppet returns.

If the children really want to personally interact with the puppet, try to create a time when it is appropriate for them to do so. Read the ideas in this section under number 5 concerning safe ways for the children to interact with the puppet. The finger-tasting idea usually satisfies their burning desire to have personal interaction with the puppet.

If the children really want to touch the puppet, have the puppet tell or show them the kind of touch it likes. It is best to allow only one child at a time to actually touch the puppet, so that the puppet can respond appropriately. In other words, a pat on the head is nice, and the puppet responds by sighing a big sigh and snuggling closer. A poke in the eye is not nice, and the puppet responds by jumping back out of reach and turning its head away to hide on your shoulder.

You may suggest touches the puppet would like, like a scratch behind the ears or under the chin, which always makes the puppet sleepy. If a child does touch the puppet in a hurtful way, causing the puppet to withdraw, explain what has happened and suggest some good touches the child could use to make friends with the puppet again.

7. Puppet Fights

Whenever my kids use puppets, they always make the puppets fight.

If children are given puppets for free play with no direction on how the puppets are to be used, the children often tend to make those puppets bite, hit, and pound on each other. This seems to be a pretty universal reaction, and it can be quite disturbing to the adult who is not expecting it. It can also be very hard on the puppets, especially delicate ones made by the children themselves.

The main antidote for this fighting phenomenon is giving the children lots of information on alternative behaviors. Many child-centered ideas are given in Section 2: Simple Puppet Activities Children Can Do.

There are also books listed in Chapter 10: Resources, giving more information on teaching puppetry to children. One of my favorites is *Making Puppets Come Alive* by Larry Engler and Carol Fijan Engler.

If you want the children to create their own stories during free play, you may wish to set a few simple rules:

a. *Puppets may not touch each other.*

They may not fight, hit, or bite. Help the children think of other things the puppets can do instead. They may look at each other, run races together, play hide-and-seek, talk to each other, surprise each other, go to sleep, look for something, act out scenes from familiar stories, etc.

b. *Only two children at a time may be in the performance area.*

This helps to prevent crowding and confusion that can lead to rough play. Other children may watch from a safe distance behind a tape line you have put on the floor to designate the audience area. After a time, the children may switch so that audience members have a turn with the puppets and the puppeteers have a chance to watch others perform.

c. *If children really need to show a fight in their story, help them plan it.*

For example, the fight between the troll and the Biggest Billy Goat Gruff is an integral part of the climax to the folktale "The Three Billy Goats Gruff."

An effective stage fight requires lots of cooperation among the players. Discuss with the children how fights are staged on TV or for the movies. The children usually know that one person pretends to strike another, stopping just short of really touching the other. The other has to cooperate to make it look like a real blow by falling backwards or reacting in some way.

Also remind the children that in a real fight action does not occur at the same hysterical rate throughout the fight. Fighters get tired, stop to rest for a second, take a long time getting up after an especially hard fall, and try to run away. Help them explore all the action possibilities. The play will be more fun, and cooperation will be fostered between players.

8. How to Use Your Puppets

I have this really cute puppet (perhaps a whole closetful of really cute puppets), and I don't know what to do with it.

Look through the activities in this book. Some of the ideas can be done with almost any hand puppet character. For example, some of the ideas on ways to use a puppet to introduce a book can be done with any puppet character able to pick up a book in its mouth or with its hands or paws.

Also see if any of the ideas in this book can be adapted to the puppet characters you already own. For example, a student of mine saw me demonstrate the song "I'm Being Eaten by a Boa Constrictor" using a very snaky sock puppet. She didn't have a snake puppet, but she had a very cute alligator with a moving mouth. She adapted the ideas in "I'm Being Eaten by a Boa Constrictor" into a new song created especially for her alligator. Her title was "I'm Being Tickled by an Alligator!" And that tooth-filled alligator mouth became the source of much tickling and giggling.

After trying some of the ideas in this book, if you'd like more activities to do with your skunk or camel or princess or martian or other special character, spend some time playing with it. Look at it in the mirror and see what it can do well. Can it turn its head to the side, wink, wiggle its ears, pick things up, or yawn?

Also observe the first impression you get of its character as you look at it. Does it look haughty, scary, silly, frightened, naive, messy, prissy, bossy, or friendly? Give yourself some time to assimilate these observations.

As you work with the children, keep this puppet character in your awareness. How could you use its special qualities and abilities to interact with the children? Do you see a story that contains some of the same qualities that the puppet could introduce? Perhaps that messy-looking puppet could help lead your cleanup time after a craft project.

Maybe your puppet could get involved in a classroom routine. This idea is demonstrated in Chapter 1, with Mortimer the Bear being a storytime helper. It's especially satisfying to involve a puppet in a project the children are tired of doing or never want to do. They may not listen to you, but they will listen to a puppet bringing new life to the activity.

Pick an idea, and then use the information you already have about how the puppet looks and what it can do to help you plan how the puppet can be involved. Be playful as you look at all the ways to use the puppet to enhance your idea.

9. Sources for Buying Puppets

Where can I buy good puppets?

Because puppets vary widely in size and in their ability to be manipulated, the best way to buy a puppet is to try it on and see how it works for you. Does it fit your hand comfortably? Is it easy to manipulate? Can you discover several things that it can easily do, like walking, looking around, eating, sleeping, hiding, or rubbing its eyes?

Because it is best to try puppets on before buying, look for puppets in local toy stores and larger department stores. If you cannot find characters you need locally, then look at Chapter 10, which lists many excellent sources for ordering puppets by mail. Be sure you can return them if they do not fit your hand or move easily.

10. Sources for Making Puppets

How can I make good puppets?

The bibliography in Chapter 10 lists many fine books on puppet making for children and adults. It also has sources to purchase some of these books by mail. Haunt your local library to see what resources they have to add to the list. Fabric stores often have a few puppet patterns for sale. Look in the novelty section of the pattern books or ask for help.

As you make the puppet, keep in mind what it must do. One time I was planning to tell "The Fisherman and His Wife," using a fish puppet. I had a wonderful time making a large, elaborate magic fish puppet, only to find that it was too big to hide behind my back as I told the story. Plan ahead and avoid those disappointments!

Most important of all, have fun. One of the most delightful puppets I've seen recently was made by one of my students, using a toilet scrubbing brush and two yellow fingers cut from a plastic glove. The puppeteer's index and middle fingers, wearing the yellow glove fingers, protruded through the center opening of the round brush to become the puppet's mouth. The puppeteer simply held the brush handle in her free hand, and the puppet talked and picked things up, using its "mouth." You may have the ingredients for your best puppet friend under your sink right now!

Chapter Nine
Children's Literature Selected for Storytime Characters and Themes

The books listed below have been selected for their effectiveness in storytime presentations. They are grouped by the themes represented in the scripts found in Sections 1 and 2. You may use this list to assist you in choosing books on a theme to use in storytime along with a puppet presentation. You may also use this section to find additional stories to tell, using the puppet characters you purchase or create for the scripts found in this book. The listings below include age-level suggestions.

Bears

Use with "The Bear Went Over the Mountain," "The Boy and the Bear," and "Lizard's Song."

Asch, Frank. *Bear Shadow*. Englewood Cliffs, NJ: Prentice-Hall, 1985. Ages: 3 to 7.

Chambless, Jane. *Tucker and the Bear*. New York: Simon and Schuster Books for Young Readers, 1989. Ages: 6 to 8.

Fox, Mem. *Koala Lou*. Illustrated by Pamela Lofts. San Diego: Harcourt Brace Jovanovich, 1988. Ages: 3 to 7.

Kennedy, Jimmy. *The Teddy Bears' Picnic*. Illustrated by Prue Theobalds. New York: P. Bedrick Books, 1987. Ages: 2 to 7.

Martin, B. *Brown Bear, Brown Bear, What Do You See?* Illustrated by Eric Carle. New York: Holt, Rinehart, and Winston, 1983. Ages: 2 to 5.

Myers, Bernice. *Not This Bear!* New York: Four Winds Press, 1968. Ages: 5 to 8.

Riddell, Chris. *The Bear Dance*. New York: Simon and Schuster Books for Young Readers, 1990. Ages: 5 to 7.

Weiss, Nicki. *Where Does the Brown Bear Go?* New York: Greenwillow Books, 1989. Ages: 2 to 5.

Chickens

Use with "Something to Crow About" and "The Little Red Hen and the Grain of Wheat."

Carle, Eric. *Rooster's Off to See the World*. Natick, ME: Picture Book Studio, 1972. Ages: 3 to 5.

Heine, Helme. *The Most Wonderful Egg in the World*. New York: Atheneum, 1983. Ages: 3 to 7.

Hutchins, Pat. *Rosie's Walk*. New York: Macmillan, 1968. Ages: 3 to 5.

Marshall, James. *Wings: A Tale of Two Chickens*. New York: Viking Kestrel, 1986. Ages: 6 to 8.

Roy, Ron. *Three Ducks Went Wandering*. Illustrated by Paul Galdone. New York: Seabury Press, 1979. Ages: 3 to 5.

Saunders, Dave and Julie Saunders. *Dibble and Dabble*. New York: Bradbury Press, 1990. Ages: 2 to 5.

Stehr, Frederic. *Quack-quack*. New York: Farrar, Straus and Giroux, 1987. Ages: 3 to 5.

Clothes

Use with "Getting Dressed for Storytime" and "Who Took the Farmer's Hat?"

dePaola, Thomas Anthony. *Charlie Needs a Cloak*. Englewood Cliffs, NJ: Prentice-Hall, 1973. Ages: 4 to 7.

Fox, Mem. *Shoes from Grandpa*. Illustrated by Patricia Mullins. New York: Orchard Books, 1989. Ages: 4 to 7.

Hutchins, Pat. *You'll Soon Grow Into Them, Titch*. New York: Greenwillow Books, 1983. Ages: 2 to 5.

Leemis, Ralph. *Mister Momboo's Hat*. Illustrations by Jeni Bassett. New York: Dutton, 1991. Ages: 2 to 5.

Rockwell, Anne F. *First Comes Spring*. New York: T.Y. Crowell, 1985. Ages: 3 to 5.

Slobodkina, Esphyr. *Caps for Sale*. New York: W.R. Scott, 1947. Ages: 2 to 6.

Watanabe, Shigeo. *How Do I Put It On?* New York: Philomel Books, 1977. Ages: 2 to 4.

Wells, Rosemary. *Max's Dragon Shirt.* New York: Dial Books for Young Readers, 1991. Ages: 2 to 5.

Yektai, Niki. *Crazy Clothes.* Illustrated by Su,cie Stevenson. New York: Bradbury Press, 1988. Ages: 3 to 5.

Ecology

Use with "Nine-in-One, Grr! Grr!," "You Can't Make a Turtle Come Out," "The Boy and the Bear," "The Very Busy Spider," "Wide-Mouthed Frog," and "Bad Habits."

All in This Together: 15 Ecology Songs for the Whole Family features The Singing Rainbows, ages nine through fifteen, with other fine musicians in folk, jazz, and rock numbers about the disappearing rain forest, pet overpopulation, endangered species, etc. The songs are by Nancy Schimmel and Candy Forest. Order from Sisters' Choice Press, 1450 Sixth Street, Berkeley, CA 94710. (510) 524-5804.

Baylor, Byrd. *Everybody Needs a Rock.* Illustrated by Peter Parnall. New York: Scribner, 1974. Ages: 6 to 8.

Lionni, Leo. *A Color of His Own.* New York: Pantheon Books, 1975. Ages: 2 to 5.

Marzollo, Jean. *Pretend You're a Cat.* Illustrated by Jerry Pinkney. New York: Dial Books for Young Readers, 1990. Ages: 2 to 5.

Mazer, Anne. *The Salamander Room.* Illustrated by Steve Johnson. New York: Knopf, 1991. Ages: 4 to 8.

Mizumura, Kazue. *If I Built a Village. . .* New York: Thomas Y. Crowell Company, 1971. Ages: 4 to 7.

Scheffler, Ursel. *Stop Your Crowing, Kasmir!* Illustrated by Silke Brix-Henker. Minneapolis: Carolrhoda Books, 1986. Ages: 5 to 8.

Yolen, Jane. *Owl Moon.* Illustrated by John Schoenherr. New York: Philomel Books, 1987. Ages: 5 to 8.

Families

Use with "Pierre" and "The Three Billy Goats Gruff."

Bunting, Eve. *No Nap.* Illustrated by Susan Meddaugh. New York: Clarion Books, 1989. Ages: 3 to 5.

Carson, Jo. *Pulling My Leg.* Illustrated by Julie Downing. New York: Orchard Books, 1990. Ages: 5 to 7.

Douglass, Barbara. *Good as New.* Illustrated by Patience Brewster. New York: Lothrop, Lee & Shepard Books, 1982. Ages: 4 to 7.

Friedman, Ina R. *How My Parents Learned to Eat.* Illustrated by Allen Say. Boston: Houghton Mifflin, 1984. Ages: 6 to 8.

Galbraith, Kathryn Osebold. *Laura Charlotte.* Illustrated by Floyd Cooper. New York: Philomel Books, 1990. Ages: 5 to 8.

Grifalconi, Ann. *The Village of Round and Square Houses.* Boston: Little, Brown, 1986. Ages: 6 to 8.

Hines, Anna Grossnickle. *Big Like Me.* New York: Greenwillow Books, 1989. Ages: 3 to 5.

Hutchins, Pat. *Where's the Baby?* New York: Greenwillow Books, 1988. Ages: 3 to 5.

Kamen, Gloria. *"Paddle," Said the Swan.* New York: Atheneum, 1989. Ages: 2 to 4.

Keller, Holly. *Horace.* New York: Greenwillow Books, 1991. Ages: 3 to 5.

Mahy, Margaret. *The Seven Chinese Brothers.* Illustrated by Jean and Mou-sien Tseng. New York: Scholastic, Inc., 1990. Ages: 5 to 8.

Rees, Mary. *Ten in a Bed.* Boston: Little, Brown and Company, 1988. Ages: 3 to 5.

Stolz, Mary. *Storm in the Night.* Illustrated by Pat Cummings. New York: Harper and Row, 1988. Ages: 5 to 8.

Williams, Vera B. *"More More More," Said the Baby: Three Love Stories.* New York: Greenwillow Books, 1990. Ages: 2 to 5.

Wishinsky, Frieda. *Oonga Boonga.* Illustrated by Su,cie Stevenson. Boston: Little, Brown, 1990. Ages: 3 to 6.

Food

Use with the "Peanut Butter/Jelly!" song, "I Know an Old Lady Who Swallowed a Fly," "The Little Red Hen and the Grain of Wheat," "Wide-Mouthed Frog," "The Teeny Tiny Woman," and "The Three Billy Goats Gruff."

Carle, Eric. *The Very Hungry Caterpillar.* New York: Philomel Books, 1987. Ages: 2 to 5.

Carrick, Donald. *Milk.* New York: Greenwillow Books, 1985. Ages: 3 to 5.

Ehlert, Lois. *Feathers for Lunch.* San Diego: Harcourt Brace Jovanovich, 1990. Ages: 3 to 7.

———. *Growing Vegetable Soup.* San Diego: Harcourt Brace Jovanovich, 1987. Ages: 2 to 7.

Galdone, Paul. *The Magic Porridge Pot.* New York: Houghton Mifflin, 1976. Ages: 5 to 8.

Hennessy, B.G. *Jake Baked the Cake.* Illustrated by Mary Morgan. New York: Viking Penguin, 1990. Ages: 2 to 5.

Jameson, Cynthia. *The Clay Pot Boy.* Illustrated by Arnold Lobel. New York: Coward, McCann & Geoghegan, Inc., 1973. Ages: 3 to 7.

Numeroff, Laura Joffe. *If You Give a Mouse a Cookie.* Illustrated by Felicia Bond. New York: Harper & Row, 1985. Ages: 2 to 6.

Polette, Nancy. *The Little Old Woman and the Hungry Cat.* Illustrated by Frank Modell. New York: Greenwillow Books, 1989.

Sloat, Teri. *The Eye of the Needle.* New York: Dutton, 1990. Ages: 5 to 8.

Titherington, Jeanne. *Pumpkin Pumpkin.* New York: Greenwillow Books, 1986. Ages: 2 to 5.

Vaughan, Marcia K. *Wombat Stew.* Illustrated by Pamela Lofts. Morristown, NJ: Silver Burdett Company, 1984. Ages: 5 to 8.

Westcott, Nadine Bernard. *Peanut Butter and Jelly: A Play Rhyme.* New York: E.P. Dutton, 1987. Ages: 2 to 8.

Friends

Use with "The Boy and the Bear," "Lizard's Song," "The Little Red Hen and the Grain of Wheat," and "Bad Habits."

Fox, Mem. *Wilfrid Gordon McDonald Partridge.* Illustrated by Julie Vivas. Brooklyn, NY: Kane/Miller Book Publishers, 1984. Ages: 4 to 7.

Rylant, Cynthia. *Mr. Griggs' Work.* Illustrated by Julie Downing. New York: Orchard Books, 1989. Ages: 5 to 8.

Wild, Margaret. *Mr. Nick's Knitting.* Illustrated by Dee Huxley. San Diego: Harcourt Brace Jovanovich, 1989. Ages: 4 to 7.

Frogs

Use with "Wide-Mouthed Frog."

Berenzy, Alix. *A Frog Prince.* New York: H. Holt, 1989. Ages: 6 to 8.

Priceman, Marjorie. *Friend or Frog.* Boston: Houghton Mifflin, 1989. Ages: 6 to 8.

Scieszka, Jon. *The Frog Prince Continued.* Illustrated by Steve Johnson. New York: Viking, 1991. Ages: 6 to 8.

Humor

Use with the "Peanut Butter/Jelly!" song, "I Know an Old Lady Who Swallowed a Fly," "Pierre," "Bad Habits," and "Wide-Mouthed Frog."

Allard, Harry and James Marshall. *Miss Nelson Is Back.* Boston: Houghton Mifflin, 1982. Ages: 6 to 8.

———. *Miss Nelson Is Missing!* Boston: Houghton Mifflin, 1977. Ages: 6 to 8.

Mahy, Margaret. *The Pumpkin Man and the Crafty Creeper.* Illustrated by Helen Craig. New York: Lothrop, Lee & Shepard Books, 1990. Ages: 6 to 8.

Marshall, Edward. *Space Case.* New York: Dial, 1980. Ages: 5 to 8.

Yorinks, Arthur. *Company's Coming.* Illustrated by David Small. New York: Crown Publishers, 1988. Ages: 6 to 8.

Imagination

Use with "I Know an Old Lady Who Swallowed a Fly," "The Little Pot," and "Where the Wild Things Are."

Agee, John. *The Incredible Painting of Felix Clousseau.* New York: Farrar, Straus, & Giroux, 1988. Ages: 6 to 8.

Burningham, John. *John Patrick Norman McHennessy: The Boy Who Was Always Late.* New York: Crown, 1987. Ages: 6 to 8.

Martin, Bill and John Archambault. *Barn Dance!* Illustrated by Ted Rand. New York: H. Holt, 1986. Ages: 5 to 7.

Martin, Rafe. *Will's Mammoth.* Illustrated by Stephen Gammell. New York: Putnam's, 1989. Ages: 3 to 5.

Morgan, Michaela. *Visitors for Edward.* Illustrated by Sue Porter. New York: E.P. Dutton, 1987. Ages: 4 to 6.

Ueno, Noriko. *Elephant Buttons.* New York: Harper & Row, 1973. Ages: 3 to 5.

Jungle Beasts

Use with "Bad Habits," "Wide-Mouthed Frog," "The Tortoise and the Hare," "Pierre," and "Nine-in-One, Grr! Grr!"

Aardema, Verna. *Who's in Rabbit's House?* Illustrated by Leo and Diane Dillon. New York: Dial Press, 1977. Ages: 5 to 8.

Drescher, Henrik. *Whose Scaly Tail?* New York: Lippincott, 1987. Ages: 2 to 5.

Emberley, Rebecca. *Jungle Sounds.* Boston: Little, Brown, 1989. Ages: 3 to 5.

Jorgensen, Gail. *Crocodile Beat.* Illustrated by Patricia Mullins. New York: Bradbury Press, 1989. Ages: 3 to 5.

Maestro, Betsy and Giulio Maestro. *A Wise Monkey Tale.* New York: Crown Publishers, Inc. Ages: 5 to 8.

Martin, Rafe. *Foolish Rabbit's Big Mistake.* Illustrated by Ed Young. New York: Putnam, 1985. Ages: 5 to 8.

Tafuri, Nancy. *Junglewalk.* New York: Greenwillow Books, 1988. Ages: 3 to 5.

Perseverance

Use with "The Tortoise and the Hare."

Hutchins, Pat. *Titch.* New York: The Macmillan Company, 1971. Ages: 2 to 5.

Keats, Ezra Jack. *Whistle for Willie.* New York: The Viking Press, 1964. Ages: 3 to 5.

Sanders, Scott Russell. *Aurora Means Dawn.* Illustrated by Jill Kastner. New York: Bradbury Press, 1989. Ages: 6 to 8.

Stevenson, James. *"Could Be Worse!"* New York: Greenwillow, 1977. Ages: 5 to 8.

Tolstoy, Alexei. *The Great Big Enormous Turnip.* Illustrated by Helen Oxenbury. New York: Watts, 1968. Ages: 2 to 5.

Pigs

Use with "The Three Little Pigs."

Gackenbach, Dick. *Harvey, the Foolish Pig.* New York: Clarion Books, 1988. Ages: 6 to 8.

Gretz, Suzanna. *Roger Takes Charge!* New York: Dial Books for Young Readers, 1987. Ages 3 to 6.

Kasza, Keiko. *The Pig's Picnic.* New York: Putnam, 1988. Ages: 4 to 7.

McPhail, David. *Pig Pig Goes to Camp.* New York: Dutton, 1983. Ages: 4 to 7.

Ross, Tony. *The Three Pigs.* New York: Pantheon Books, 1983. Ages: 6 to 8.

Scary Creatures

Use with "The Little Old Lady Who Was Not Afraid of Anything," "The Teeny Tiny Woman," "The Three Billy Goats Gruff," "The Gunny Wolf," "Pierre," and "Where the Wild Things Are."

Balian, Lorna. *The Aminal.* Nashville: Abingdon Press, 1976. Ages: 4 to 8.

dePaola, Tomie. *The Knight and the Dragon.* New York: G.P. Putnam's Sons, 1980. Ages: 6 to 8.

Hodges, Margaret. *Buried Moon.* Boston: Little, Brown, 1990. Ages: 6 to 8.

Howe, John. *Jack and the Beanstalk.* Boston: Little, Brown, 1989. Ages: 5 to 8.

Martin, Bill and John Archainbault. *The Ghost-eye Tree.* Illustrated by Ted Rand. New York: Holt, Rinehart and Winston, 1985. Ages: 6 to 8.

Mayer, Mercer. *There's a Nightmare in My Closet.* New York: Dial Books for Young Readers, 1968. Ages: 2 to 5.

McQueen, John Troy. *A World Full of Monsters.* Illustrated by Marc Brown. New York: Crowell, 1986. Ages: 3 to 6.

Riley, James Whitcombe. *The Gobble-Uns'll Git You Ef You Don't Watch Out!* Illustrated by Joel Schick. Philadelphia: Lippincott. Ages: 6 to 8.

Seeger, Pete. *Abiyoyo: South African Lullaby and Folk Story.* Illustrated by Michael Hays. New York: Macmillan, 1986. Ages: 4 to 8.

Viorst, Judith. *My Mama Says There Aren't Any Zombies, Ghosts, Vampires, Creatures, Demons, Monsters, Fiends, Goblins, or Things.* Illustrated by Kay Chorao. New York: Atheneum, 1984. Ages: 5 to 7.

Zemach, Harve. *The Judge.* Illustrated by Margot Zemach. New York: Farrar, Straus & Giroux, 1969. Ages: 6 to 8.

Self-esteem

Use with "Something to Crow About," "Lizard's Song," and "The Little Old Lady Who Was Not Afraid of Anything."

Baker, Keith. *The Magic Fan.* San Diego: Harcourt Brace Jovanovich, 1989. Ages: 6 to 8.

Cohen, Miriam. *So What?* Illustrated by Lillian Hoban. New York: Greenwillow, 1982. Ages: 5 to 7.

DeRegniers, Beatrice Schenk. *Everyone Is Good for Something.* New York: Houghton Mifflin, 1980. Ages: 6 to 8.

DeVeaux, Alexis. *An Enchanted Hair Tale.* Illustrated by Cheryl Hanna. New York: Harper & Row, 1987. Ages: 6 to 8.

Keats, Ezra Jack. *Regards to the Man in the Moon.* New York: Four Winds Press, 1981. Ages: 5 to 7.

Pinkwater, Manus. *The Big Orange Splot.* New York: Hastings, 1977. Ages 5 to 8.

Surprises

Use with "Donna O'Neeshuck Was Chased by Some Cows," "The Little Old Lady Who Was Not Afraid of Anything," "Nine in One, Grr! Grr!," "The Boy and the Bear," "The Teeny Tiny Woman," "The Little Pot," and "Pierre."

Aylesworth, Jim. *Shenandoah Noah.* Illustrated by Glen Rounds. New York: Holt, Rinehart, and Winston, 1985. Ages: 6 to 8.

Charlip, Remy. *Fortunately.* New York: Parents' Magazine Press, 1964. Ages: 3 to 8.

Cole, Babette. *The Trouble with Gran.* New York: Putnam, 1987. Ages: 6 to 8. (See also *The Trouble with Mom* and *The Trouble with Dad.*)

Gammell, Stephen. *Once Upon MacDonald's Farm.* New York: Four Winds Press, 1981. Ages: 4 to 8.

Gross, Ruth Belov. *The Girl Who Wouldn't Get Married.* Illustrated by Jack Kent. New York: Four Winds Press, 1983. Ages: 7 to 8.

Kimmel, Eric A. *Four Dollars and Fifty Cents*. Illustrated by Glen Rounds. New York: Holiday House, 1990. Ages: 6 to 8.

MacDonald, Amy. *Rachel Fister's Blister*. Illustrated by Marjorie Priceman. Boston: Houghton Mifflin, 1990. Ages: 5 to 7.

Mahy, Margaret. *The Great White Man-Eating Shark: A Cautionary Tale*. Illustrated by Jonathan Allen. New York: Dial Books for Young Readers, 1989. Ages: 7 & 8.

Myers, Bernice. *Sidney Rella and the Glass Sneaker*. New York: Macmillan, 1985. Ages: 7 & 8.

Small, David. *Imogene's Antlers*. New York: Crown Publishers, Inc., 1985. Ages: 5 to 8.

Stamm, Claus. *Three Strong Women: A Tall Tale from Japan*. Illustrated by Jen Tseng and Mou-sien Tseng. New York: Viking, 1990. Ages: 6 to 8.

Wood, Don and Audrey Wood. *The Little Mouse, the Red Ripe Strawberry, and the Big Hungry Bear*. England: Child's Play (International), 1984. Ages: 3 to 5.

Zemach, Harve. *A Penny a Look*. Illustrated by Margot Zemach. New York: Farrar, Straus, & Giroux, 1971. Ages: 6 to 8.

Zemach, Margot. *The Three Wishes: An Old Story*. New York: Farrar, Straus, & Giroux, 1986. Ages: 4 to 8.

Turtles

Use with "You Can't Make a Turtle Come Out" and "The Tortoise and the Hare."

Asch, Frank. *Turtle Tale*. New York: Dial Press, 1978. Ages: 2 to 5.

Baylor, Byrd. *Desert Voices*. Illustrated by Peter Parnall. New York: Scribner, 1981. Ages: 7 & 8.

Bryan, Ashley. *Turtle Knows Your Name*. New York: Atheneum, 1989. Ages: 6 to 8.

Collins, Pat Lowery. *Tomorrow, Up and Away!* Illustrated by Lynn Munsinger. Boston: Houghton Mifflin, 1990. Ages: 3 to 6.

Florian, Douglas. *Turtle Day*. New York: Crowell, 1989. Ages: 3 to 5.

George, William T. *Box Turtle at Long Pond*. Illustrated by Lindsay Barrett George. New York: Greenwillow Books, 1989. Ages: 5 to 7.

Maris, Ron. *I Wish I Could Fly*. New York: Greenwillow Books, 1986. Ages: 2 to 5.

Williams, Barbara. *Albert's Toothache*. Illustrated by Kay Chorao. New York: Dutton, 1974. Ages: 4 to 7.

Yashima, Taro, pseud. *Seashore Story*. New York: The Viking Press, 1967. Ages: 6 to 8.

Wolves

Use with "The Gunny Wolf" and "The Three Little Pigs."

Kasza, Keiko. *The Wolf's Chicken Stew*. New York: Putnam, 1987. Ages: 2 to 6.

Marshall, James. *Red Riding Hood*. New York: Dial Books for Young Readers, 1987. Ages: 5 to 8.

Scieszka, Jon. *The True Story of the 3 Little Pigs; by A. Wolf as told to Jon Scieszka*. Illustrated by Lane Smith. New York: Viking Kestrel, 1989. Ages: 6 to 8.

Chapter Ten
Resources

SOURCES FOR PURCHASING PUPPETS

The following resources specialize in puppets and puppet products. They offer some of the puppet characters found in the scripts in this book. You will want to write for several catalogs, as the catalogs represent a wide range of puppet styles and prices. See Chapter 8 under "Where can I buy good puppets?" for information on choosing puppets.

Dorothy Tharpe, 73 East Terresa St., Roberts, WI 54023.

Reasonably priced finger puppets perfect for storytelling to small groups. Storytelling sets for "Chicken Little," "Goldilocks and the Three Bears," "Three Billy Goats Gruff," "Gingerbread Man," "Fisherman and His Wife," "Little Red Riding Hood," "Hansel and Gretel," and "Frog Prince" are available. You can also buy single puppet characters, including a teeny tiny woman, and a book of knitting patterns to make your own.

Heartcraft Puppets, Sunny Stansbury, P.O. Box 1730, Corrales, NM 87048.

If you wish to make your own simple animal hand puppets, order this pattern set. It includes patterns for a lizard, turtle, eagle, wolf, coyote, rabbit, and deer.

Joyce Anderson, 138 Belvale Dr., Los Gatos, CA 95032.

A large selection of well-made, reasonably priced pop-up puppet characters—including bird, clown, bear, pig, boy, girl, troll, cow, frog, and dragon—are available.

Langtry Publications, 7838 Burnet Ave., Van Nuys, CA 91405-1051. FAX (818) 988-0037.

More than one hundred hand and finger puppets, including holiday, animal, and people puppets, are available from this company.

MasterCraft Puppets, P.O. Box 309, Branson, MO 65616.

Besides offering a large selection of ready-made puppets, they will make custom puppets on request.

Monkey Merchant, Inc., 326 West Eleventh St., National City, CA 91950. (619) 477-1180.

Their flyer advertises hand puppets in two sizes, as well as a few finger puppets. Hand puppets include cow, dog, bear, pig, goat, and rabbit. Finger puppets include pig, rabbit, longhorn steer, and red hen.

Nancy Renfro Studios, P.O. Box 164226, Austin, TX 78716. 1-800-933-5512. FAX (512) 327-9588.

Puppets and puppet-related products, including books and puppets for the special child, are available from this resource.

Poppets, 3124 Elliott Ave., Seattle, WA 98121. (206) 285-3107.

This catalog includes a selection of brightly colored hand puppets.

Puppet Productions, P.O. Box 1066, DeSoto, TX 75123-1066. 1-800-854-2151.

This company offers very large puppets with moving mouths. They have a wide selection of people puppets and a few animal puppets.

Puppets on the Pier, Pier 39, Box H-4, San Francisco, CA 94133. 1-800-443-4463.

This puppet store is open 364 days of the year and ships worldwide. They offer more than 500 different puppets and are willing to search for a particular character if you have a special need.

WatchMe Blossom Theatre Works, 109 SE Alder, Portland, OR 97214. (503) 231-8469. FAX (503) 243-6815.

Puppets, puppet stages, and puppet books are available from this company.

The following catalogs carry a few puppets and puppet stages as parts of their product line.

Childcraft
P.O. Box 29149
Mission, KS 66201-9149
1-800-631-5657   FAX (913) 752-1095

HearthSong
P.O. Box B
Sebastopol, CA 95473-0601
1-800-325-2502   FAX 1-800-872-0331

Kaplan School Supply Corp.
Eastern Headquarters
1310 Lewisville-Clemmons Road
Lewisville, NC 27023
1-800-334-2014 (US)   1-800-642-0610 (NC)

Kids & Things
P.O. Box 7488
Madison, WI 53707
1-800-356-1200

Western Headquarters
5360 Eastgate Mall, Suite E
San Diego, CA 92121
1-800-433-1591 (CA)

Lakeshore Curriculum Materials Company
P.O. Box 6261
Carson, CA 90749
1-800-421-5354

PUPPETRY AND STORYTELLING
A SELECTED BIBLIOGRAPHY

Baird, Bill. *The Art of the Puppet*. New York: Crown, 1973.
International history of puppetry with beautiful photographs. Shows puppetry in a cultural context.

Chernoff, Goldie Taub. *Puppet Party*. New York: Walker, 1971.
Useful to inspire children to make puppets on their own. Simple construction methods visually and colorfully presented.

Dean, Audrey. *Puppets That Are Different*. New York: Taplinger, 1974.
For adults who wish to make long-lasting, attractive cloth puppets. Includes a dragon, a snake charmer, a lion, and a horse.

Engler, Larry and Carol Fijan. *Making Puppets Come Alive*. New York: Taplinger, 1973.
Excellent manual of hand puppet manipulation. Offers concrete suggestions for teaching puppetry and putting on a show.

Farrell, Catharine Horne. *Word Weaving: A Guide to Storytelling*. Zellerbach Family Fund, 1983.
A simple, practical guide to becoming a storyteller.

Flower, Cedric and Alan Jon Fortney. *Puppets: Methods and Materials*. Worcester, MA: Davis Publications, Inc., 1983.
For the adult who wants to know more about puppets, this book covers shadow puppets, hand puppets, rod puppets, and marionettes as well as puppet stages and puppet design.
Howard, Vernon. *Puppets and Pantomime Plays*. Rev. ed. New York: Sterling Publishing Company, 1969.
Provides guidance for creating original skits and plays. Encourages experimentation and creativity.

Hunt, Tamara and Nancy Renfro. *Puppetry in Early Childhood Education*. Austin, TX: Nancy Renfro Studios, 1982.
An excellent, comprehensive resource on the subject. Includes patterns for puppet making and a wealth of ideas on using puppets with preschoolers.

Maguire, Jack. *Creative Storytelling: Choosing, Inventing, and Sharing Tales for Children*. New York: McGraw-Hill Book Company, 1985.
Covers the value of storytelling and how to do it, with encouragement for creating your own stories.

Renfro, Nancy. *Puppetry and the Art of Story Creation*. Austin, TX: Nancy Renfro Studios, 1979.
Especially helpful for script writing. Also includes lots of ideas on creating simple puppets and a section on puppetry for the physically disabled and the hearing and visually impaired.

Rottman, Fran. *Easy to Make Puppets and How to Use Them: Early Childhood*. Glendale: G/L Publications, 1978.
This paperback is full of ideas for making simple puppets, including some patterns. It is of special interest to people working with toddlers through age five. Rottman has also written a book called *Easy to Make Puppets and How to Use Them: Childhood and Youth*, which is for children ages six and up, so be sure to get the age level you want. Both of these books include Bible stories as well as lots of basic puppet information.

Schimmel, Nancy. *Just Enough to Make a Story: A Sourcebook for Storytelling*. Rev. ed. Berkeley, CA: Sisters' Choice Press, 1982.
Gives tips on choosing, learning, and telling a story. Helpful bibliographies, including Active Heroines in Folktales for Children, Peace Stories, and Ecology Stories.

Sierra, Judy. *Fantastic Theater: Puppets and Plays for Young Performers and Young Audiences*. Bronx, New York, H.W. Wilson Company, 1991.
This practical book contains 30 plays with puppet patterns. The plays are derived from poetry, traditional folk songs, fables, folktales, and myths. They are designed to be performed by children or by adults for a child audience, and directions are provided for both shadow and rod puppet productions. Many of these will work well with young children.

_____. *The Flannel Board Storytelling Book*. Bronx, NY: H.W. Wilson Company, 1987.
Thirty-six well-chosen stories, poems, and songs for use with children ages three to eight. More than 250 flannel board patterns are included; these could be patterns for stick puppets as well.

Sierra, Judy and Robert Kaminski. *Multicultural Folktales: Stories to Tell Young Children*. Phoenix: Oryx Press, 1991.

Many of these stories, chosen for children ages two and a half to seven, provide excellent material for storytelling with puppets and other simple puppet activities.

Sylwester, Roland. *Teaching Bible Stories More Effectively with Puppets.* St. Louis: Concordia Publishing House, 1976.

Although the emphasis is on Bible stories, this inexpensive book is a great introduction to puppetry for any purpose.

PUPPETRY ORGANIZATIONS

The Puppeteers of America
Membership Office
#5 Cricklewood Path
Pasadena, CA 91107

P of A is the national organization of puppeteers. Benefits of membership include the following:

1. The quarterly <u>Puppetry Journal</u> which discusses all aspects of puppetry, from educational puppetry to articles of interest to professional puppeteers.
2. Access to the free services of consultants with expertise in all aspects of puppetry, including puppet construction, script writing, storytelling with puppets, theatres, lighting, sound systems, etc.
3. Access to a large library of videotapes on many aspects of puppetry. Members can request to borrow up to three videos at a time which will be mailed to them for a $15.00 fee.
4. Access to The Puppetry Store, a mail order house for P of A members specializing in books on puppetry for all levels and purposes, including puppet construction, educational puppetry, religious puppetry, and puppet history and culture.
5. Information on upcoming puppet festivals and conferences all over the United States.
6. A listing of the members by state so you can find others in your area who are also interested in puppetry.

UNIMA-U.S.A., Inc.
Allelu Kurten, General Secretary
Browning Road
Hyde Park, NY 12538

This is the international equivalent of Puppeteers of America, linking Americans to puppeteers in over sixty countries. Benefits of membership include:

1. A subscription to *A Propos*, official publication of UNIMA-U.S.A., published twice yearly.

2. A calendar of world puppet festivals.
3. An annual directory of all members.
4. Access to a scholarship fund for advanced training to qualified American puppeteers.
5. Information about the International Congress and Festival held every four years in different parts of the world.

STORYTELLING RESOURCES—ASSOCIATIONS, CENTERS, CATALOGS, AND NEWSLETTERS

Good storytelling skills are a necessity for people interested in using puppets to tell stories. Storytelling organizations, newsletters, associations, and centers are listed here to assist you in learning more about the art of storytelling.

National Association

National Association for the Preservation and Perpetuation of Storytelling (NAPPS)
NAPPS
P.O. Box 309
Jonesborough, TN 37659

This is the national association for storytellers and people interested in storytelling. NAPPS has two levels of membership.

Benefits of Membership for $25.00 include the following:

1. The quarterly *Storytelling Magazine,* containing articles on such diverse topics as healing stories, true stories of the integration movement, and stories to make math education more fun.
2. News of all NAPPS activities, including the National Storytelling Festival.
3. *The Catalog of Storytelling Resources,* a treasury of storytelling books, cassettes, and materials that can be bought by mail.
4. Discounts to the National Storytelling Institute and the National Congress on Storytelling.

Benefits of Membership Plus for $40 include all the benefits listed above plus:

1. Eight issues of the <u>Yarnspinner</u> newsletter.
2. The annual *National Directory of Storytelling*, a listing of storytellers, organizations and centers, events, publications, educational opportunities, and resources.

Specialized Associations and Centers

Association of Black Storytellers, Inc. (ABS)
P.O. Box 27456
Philadelphia, PA 19118

Regular membership is $20.00. The objectives of the organization are to train and develop the skills of people interested in the art of storytelling; be a unifying force in the field of Black storytelling; establish and maintain a network of individuals and groups to keep the African oral tradition alive; establish a storytelling information and resource center; organize and conduct conferences and workshops; organize and conduct a national festival; and publish a newsletter.

The Jewish Storytelling Center
92nd St. Y Library
1395 Lexington Avenue
New York, NY 10128

Membership in The Jewish Storytelling Center is $42.00 for a 12-month period, including all meetings, full Y Library privileges, discounts to Library-sponsored storytelling events, and the *Jewish Storytelling Newsletter.*

Newsletter subscription is $10.00 for a 12-month period. The quarterly newsletter features news and calendar of storytelling events; brief tales; resources: books and recordings; discussion articles; and reports on storytelling festivals and conferences.

Catalogs and Stores

California Storytellers Catalog
Sandra MacLees
6695 Westside Road
Healdsburg, CA 95448
(707) 433-8728

Books, tapes, videos, calendars, and T-shirts for storytellers.

Spellbinders Gallery
4070 Burton Drive #2
Cambria, CA 93428
(805) 927-3385
(800) 244-2218

Book gallery featuring award-winning children's literature, folklore, mythology, and resources for storytelling.

Storylines
P.O. Box 7416
Saint Paul, MN 55107
(612) 643-4321

Mail order catalog for storytelling books, cassettes, T-shirts, games, jewelry, puppets, and related paraphernalia.

Newsletters and Local or Regional Associations

There are many newsletters of interest to storytellers being published today. Some are local or regional in focus, and some are national in scope. Listed below is a sampling of the newsletters available.

Story Street, USA
5025 Occidental Rd.
Santa Rosa, CA 95401

The Inside Story is a quarterly, national storytelling newsletter designed especially for classroom teachers, librarians, and reading specialists.

Jewish Storytelling Newsletter. See listing under The Jewish Storytelling Center for contents and costs.

Seattle Storytellers' Guild
P.O. Box 45532
Seattle, WA 98145-0532

This newsletter includes a few articles of general interest to storytellers as well as news of local and regional events.

Stories: A Western Storytelling Newsletter
Katy Rydell
12600 Woodbine Street
Los Angeles, CA 90066

Pubished quarterly, this newsletter includes articles of general interest to storytellers as well as information on storytelling events and conferences, mostly in the western states.

The Story Bag Newsletter
Harlynne Geisler, Editor
5361 Javier Street
San Diego, CA 92117-3215

This bi-monthly newsletter is full of ideas, letters, tips, professional dialogue, and advice for storytellers.

Storyline
c/o Kate Frankel
#1 Rochdale Way
Berkeley, CA 94708

A publication of the Bay Area Storytelling Festival Committee, this quarterly newsletter contains mostly local and regional news. It also reviews books and tapes and gives storytelling advice to readers' questions in a delightful "Dear Kate" column.

Tellers of Tales
9020 E. Saddleback Dr.
Tucson, AZ 85749

This newsletter includes mostly local and regional events and news.

Tennessee Storytelling Journal
ETSU Storytelling Master's Degree Program
Dr. Flora Joy, TSJ Editor and Program Sponsor
ETSU Box 21910A
Johnson City, TN 37614

Published in June and December, this journal contains stories and information about storytelling. The annual subscription rate is $7.95.

The Vancouver Storytelling Circle Newsletter
4143 W. 15th Ave.
Vancouver, BC, V6R 3A4

Published four times a year, this newsletter includes mostly local and regional events and news.

Index

by Janet Perlman

DEC - _ 2000

DEC - _ 2000